Road Racing TECHNIQUE & TRAINING

Bonne route

Road Racing
TECHNIQUE & TRAINING

**Bernard Hinault
and Claude Genzling**

Vitesse Press
Brattleboro, Vermont

Road Racing Technique & Training was originally published in French as *Cyclisme Sur Route*, part of the book series "Sports for all," edited by Daniel Mermet. Original French edition copyright © Editions Robert Laffont S.A., Paris 1986.

Translation from the French text by Georges Herzog and Veronica Brelsford. This edition edited by Barbara George.
English edition copyright © 1988 by FPL Corporation.

Dedications:
To Martine, Mickael and Alexandre—B.H.
To Laure and Aurelia—C.G.
To Camille Letierce, enthusiastic partner—D.M.

The photos which illustrate this book come from the work of Gerard Planchenault, except for the following pages:
Presse-sports: 8, 42, 45, 59, 61 (bottom), 75, 77, 86, 98, 110, 121, 125, 129, 130, 134, 147, 203.
Agence France Presse: 61 (top).
Jean-Marc Chauvel: 161.
Jean Bibard: cover.
The drawings were designed and executed by the author, except those on pages 53, 186, 187, 190, 191 and 196, which were done by Albert.

ISBN 0-941950-13-1
Library of Congress card number 87-082146

Published by Vitesse Press
A division of FPL Corporation
P.O. Box 1886
Brattleboro, VT 05301
Manufactured in the United States of America.

table
of contents

preface to the first english edition

Originally written in French, this is a book of international importance. It details the training methods and riding techniques of the top European cyclist of the decade and of the multinational La Vie Claire team, coached by a Swiss, Paul Köchli. Attesting to the scope and significance of this information is the fact that in 1986 (the year this book was first published) a Köchli disciple and teammate of Bernard Hinault—American Greg LeMond—won the Tour de France.

Bernard Hinault was born in 1954 in Yffiniac, in the French province of Brittany. Feisty and combative both on and off the bike, he is nicknamed the Badger. During his long professional career he won the Tour de France five times, the Tour of Italy three times, and the Tour of Spain twice. He was world champion in 1980 and earned the season-long Super Prestige Pernod title for best rider four times. Time trialing is one of his specialties, and he won the prestigious Grand Prix of Nations five times. He retired at the end of the 1986 season at the age of 32.

Co-author Claude Genzling has been studying and writing about the techniques of cycling for more than 10 years and is well known in Europe for his articles in *Le Cycle* and *Miroir du Cyclisme*. He studied literature and engineering at the Ecole Polytechnique in Paris and holds a degree in architecture from the National School of Fine Arts. He is a project director for the French ministry of city planning and housing and teaches at the architecture school in Paris-La Villette. A former competitor, Genzling tests out his theories while riding his own bike, and has discussed them with many of the world's top riders.

Translators Georges Herzog and Veronica Brelsford are also cyclists. Herzog was born and grew up in France, and now lives in Boston, Mass., where he rides regularly and races occasionally. Brelsford is a runner, cyclist, and triathlete who has lived in Europe and is now a language teacher at Marlboro College in Vermont.

Barbara George
March 1988

more than a
champion

T hroughout this book the two of us will be speaking as one,
except for a few obvious passages which allow us each to
express our own personal viewpoint. But before I start I would
like to devote just a few lines to what Bernard Hinault has meant
to me over the years.

Our first encounter definitely had to do with riding technique,
yet we didn't exchange a single word that day.

It was July 21, 1978, along the time trial course that led from
Metz to Nancy, where he won the yellow jersey he would wear
all the way to the finish line for his first Tour de France victory.
I had taken up a position in the midst of some open countryside
and had been filming steadily away for hours as the riders came
by. I wanted to analyze their positions and their pedaling using
my telephoto lens.

I can still see Marc Demeyer's athletic build, outstanding for
its muscularity and aerodynamics; the too-upright position of
Jacques Bruyère, Eddy Merckx's former lieutenant; and the very
slender silhouette of Henk Lubberding, moving like a sleek grey-
hound with a fluidity that reminded me of Jacques Anquetil
emerging from the Châteaufort hills to win his first Grand Prix
of Nations at the age of 19. Minutes passed. Then suddenly,
way ahead of the expected schedule, I saw in the viewfinder
the yellow headlights of motorcycles in the distance at the top
of a long false flat, warning me of Bernard Hinault's imminent
arrival. This was confirmed by the growing excitement of the
crowd along the course.

There were still several meters of film left on the reel and as
soon as the Breton appeared—wearing the blue, white, and red
French championship jersey—I filmed him without stopping. Even
with my camera whirring away at 70 frames per second I couldn't

help but be struck by the incredible power of his pedaling and by the astonishing range of motion of his foot as it eliminated the dead spot, swinging through very quickly at the moment his knee reached its highest point.

I didn't meet Bernard Hinault until the following year when I had the pleasure of accompanying him on several rides during a Renault-Gitane team training camp in Opio in the countryside near Cannes.

The 1979 season was perhaps the most spectacular of Bernard Hinault's career. That was the year he truly attained the rank of superchampion, winning the Flèche Wallonne, the Criterium of the Dauphiné-Libéré, the Tour de France, the Grand Prix of Nations, and the Tour of Lombardy with an ease that was almost insolent. Technically he was near the peak of his art, thanks to a new riding position that had been scientifically developed. It really seemed as if there was nothing he couldn't do.

The finish of the Tour de France that year was truly extraordinary. Bernard Hinault and Joop Zoetemelk, the top two on general classification, had broken away in the Chevreuse Valley. What an unbelievable sight! Wheel to wheel—"your turn, my turn" in the language of the peloton—they came proudly barreling down the Champs-Élysées like feuding brothers. I was fortunate to have a perfect vantage point right at the finish banner. I had been closely following the changes Bernard Hinault had made in his position, and I knew the successive dimensions of his bicycles almost from memory. In the euphoria of this, his second victory, achieved with such panache, my mind began to play tricks on me. As I watched him pass the stands again and again, his saddle far back, his trunk horizontal, I felt I had assumed his identity and that it was I who was out there pedaling. But now he was all wrapped in yellow, as if the tricolors of his national championship jersey had been left behind with the endless flags that dotted the avenue. Clearly faster than Zoetemelk, Bernard Hinault took the sprint under the gaze of a bronze statue, with its team of rearing horses, in front of the sun-drenched facade of the Grand Palais. Time seemed to stand still in the midst of this great celebration.

It just so happens that the dawn of Bernard Hinault's career in 1977 coincided with the start of my own studies and research on cycling, the result of a long love affair with the sport. My career as a bicycle technician was punctuated by the Breton champion's victories, just as my adolescent cycling had been by those of Louison Bobet.

Needless to say, I was excited by the idea of writing a book on cycling technique with Bernard Hinault, especially since I had gotten to know him well enough to be sure he would be interested. Still it surprised me to learn how precisely he had analyzed his method of pedaling and of using his body to go faster than anyone else. Yes, he used his head and his legs. But he also used his head "in" his legs.

The cycling press has given the impression that Bernard Hinault is a fighter who pounds on the pedals, who crushes his bicycle with overwhelming power, who triumphs over things that would break other riders, by force of nature—a nature of which he himself speaks with quiet passion. His often sensational remarks at heated moments have reinforced this image which really sticks in the public mind.

Yet after beating Francesco Moser in the twelfth stage of his third victorious Tour of Italy—in a time trial where he averaged 49 kph—it was the same Bernard Hinault who remarked, "I won because I am an artist of the bicycle, and because I know exactly what I have to do."

The Badger, an artist?

Yes, definitely.

Why else is it said when a racer demonstrates truly impressive skills that he is "giving a recital?"

One day, as he explained to me the importance of relaxing the trunk, arms, and hands as much as possible for maximum efficiency, he made this unusual observation: "You should be able to play the piano while riding, even when climbing a mountain."

Bernard Hinault shows an irrepressible taste for giving advice like this and too bad if some of it hurts. Such statements are endearing because they show a sensitivity which has not lost its edge through the hardships of competition nor through the increasingly technological nature of bicycle racing.

The paradox of Bernard Hinault is perhaps that he appeared on the scene just when scientific research was being applied to a sport which had been very empirical until then. His untamed nature and his very earthy origins would seem to predestine him to the instinctive use of his physical strength rather than to experimentation in the laboratory, but he has nevertheless benefitted a great deal from these experiments.

Bernard Hinault has been able to combine these two sides of cycling. That's what gives a special value to his testimony, above and beyond his exceptional record of achievements.

Bravo for the artist!

Claude Genzling

introduction

Against a background of world-wide change, cycling is becoming completely transformed. On the continent and beyond it the pelotons of Europe, the cradle of cycling, are meeting those of the two Americas. It is a rare team indeed that's still strictly national. The bicycle itself—long unchanged in its apparent perfection—is undergoing a metamorphosis. This has caused a new era of record setting ever since Francesco Moser smashed the already prestigious hour record of Eddy Merckx. This metamorphosis has affected not only the racing machine. We are now seeing the appearance of bicycles "of the third kind"—off-road and other kinds of mountain bikes whose sturdy shapes and large sculptured tires strangely contradict our idea of the sport. But even these still leave room for an astonishing evolution in the BMX line, unexpected as that may seem. Who would have imagined a few years ago that the human motor would take a bicycle through such spectacular gyrations? Who would have even guessed that there could be an alternative to the elegant riding of a Fausto Coppi or a Jacques Anquetil? America has gone through this and the public has followed.

This change is not simply fashion. It's evidence that by putting scientific research to work cycling can catch up to its time. Let's not go back to Henri Desgranges, founder of the Tour de France, who set the first hour record on the track in 1893. But when Roger Riviere wiped Ercole Baldini from the records by covering 46.923 km at the Vigorelli velodrome in Milan on September 23, 1958, it's no exaggeration to say that he prepared for it essentially the same way as Oscar Egg in 1912. And it wasn't the helium he put in his tires which changed the picture a lot.

But what is truly astounding is to hear Francesco Moser declare as he got off his machine on January 19, 1984, having covered 50.808 km on the track in Mexico City, "It's not quite as demanding as the last stretch of Paris-Roubaix and I'll be ready to do it again in four days." And then to see him set yet another record on the 23rd of January with 51.151 km in an hour. This can only be explained through a radical change in training methods. The remarkable level of these two performances owes a lot to the design of the bicycle used, as well as to the Italian champion's greatness. But the repeat performance, coming only a few days after the first, owes everything to his medical preparation which was developed and programmed scientifically.

Over the last 20 years the cycling world has been a rather conservative one, compared with track and field, for example. It's only quite recently that anyone has considered that riding position and pedaling method could have an effect on the rider's output at peak effort. But throwers—shotput, discus, javelin—as well as pole vaulters and even high jumpers have long been benefitting from very exacting research on their respective techniques.

Today cycling is taking its place in the whirlwind of studies, research, and experimentation. We might add that technical knowledge is bound to develop further in the coming years, so we won't attempt to describe it in detail now.

So why this book?

We didn't conceive of it as a coaching manual. It's meant for all who love cycling, not just for a handful of specialists. This doesn't mean that an experienced rider won't find material to feed his thoughts and renew his dedication. We hope he will, anyway. Learning never truly ends for the cyclist who continues to seek to get the best out of himself.

Nor is this a do-it-yourself manual to replace the various club coaches, trainers, and medical people who are dedicated to and responsible for the development and progress of riders. Nothing can take the place of direct contact and practice on the road. Even if there are general principles they must be applied to real situations, taking each individual's aptitudes, personality, and circumstances into account.

But it isn't necessary to have a qualified coach at your disposal to take pleasure in the joys of cycling. A good racing bicycle, along with a minimum of knowledge, is enough to reach a respectable level as long as you're prepared to give a mere 10 hours a week to it.

This is why we have extensively developed the chapters on choosing equipment, on riding position, and on technique, drawing on current research and the experience of top competitors. Cycling invites a certain relationship with your body. You must acquire good technique before launching into the kind of intensive training that competition demands. It is a world where the wise venture neither alone nor blindly, especially not after a certain age.

The topics of physical preparation and of training are treated in this work in such a way as to underline one of the contradictions of our time. On the one hand are the fundamental rules of healthy living, based on common sense and proven experience. On the other, a number of discoveries resulting from the increasingly detailed analysis of biological mechanisms suggest that we are entering a new era during which man's physical and psychic potential will be greatly expanded. By engaging in a sport each of us would become his own laboratory, so to speak. Booksellers have stated that the public is more and more interested in works dedicated to the "culture" of the body. This is an interesting phenomenon that can only serve sport well as long as we keep our feet on the ground—or on our pedals—in daily life.

And yet what could be simpler than putting on your riding shorts, slipping on your jersey and gloves, lacing up your shoes, filling a bottle (not with just anything), pumping up the tires to the correct pressure, checking quickly that all is working well, and finally setting off down the road, rain or shine, with joy in your heart at the idea of putting in 100 kilometers. That's what it's all about.

Like culture, the bicycle is what's still there when everything else has been forgotten!

The authors

cycling, a technical sport

Many sports require the athlete, whether professional or amateur, to perform his task and exercise his skills using an accessory, an apparatus, or a more or less complex machine. The runner needs only his shoes, but the pole vaulter, the discus thrower, the skier, the golfer, the sailboarder, the hang glider, and the sailor are all dependent on their equipment. Without it they are just ordinary people. And these are not even the so-called "mechanical" sports, whose driving force comes not from muscles fueled by the heart but from the machine itself.

Cycling, however, is the only sport where there is such total symbiosis between man and machine, where the machine becomes an extension of the body. Feet attach to the pedals, hands grip the handlebars, pelvis perches on the hollow of the saddle (at least most of the time). The road racer is glued to his bicycle for hours, not just minutes or for a brief encounter.

If you should reply that this is also true for crosscountry skiing we would point out that skis are hardly more than oversized, elongated shoes that glide on snow, whereas the bicycle is an entirely separate machine. With its levers, cogs, ball bearings, and metal architecture it is a veritable artificial horse.

A modern-day centaur fallen from a mythological heaven, the cyclist inspires lyricism in commentators. His nature changes profoundly as he mounts his machine but perhaps more so when he gets off again. Then his streamlined and lofty style suddenly gives way to the clumsy gait of a pedestrian who has lost his feeling for contact with the ground.

Here is how Roger Bastide describes Fausto Coppi: "With his firm, stiff, and awkward feet which were somehow too big for him he was like an albatross with wings folded back perched on the bridge of a ship. He was himself only when he was on his bike. His long limbs would then turn into an unbelievable harmony of lines. More than that, there was a sort of lightness or smoothness of a divine being in his pedaling."

How beautiful they appear at the start of the Tour de France, gathering like a flock of migratory birds! They reach for the pedals with the tips of their shoes, starting off slowly, sitting upright now, laughing and chatting together, exchanging some offhand comment with a spectator, momentarily leaning on one of the barricades. Already they have left the community of ordinary mortals behind. Their leg muscles are beginning to twitch nervously as they restrain their machines to avoid hitting each other or to postpone the sudden burst which heralds their flight.

Coppi the albatross, Bahamontes the eagle of Toledo, Charly Gaul the angel of the mountain—all the winged climbers are witness to the allegory of flight which has always been cycling's trademark.

Don't the French say of a strong person that he walks "like an airplane?" Like a bird whose body is carried by the air and whose wings beat rhythmically to propel him forward, the cyclist is carried by his bicycle and his legs beat alternately in a regular motion.

And what are tires, if not cushions of air? Here is how Jacques Goddet spoke of Fausto Coppi in *L'Équipe* the day after his fabulous victory in Paris-Roubaix in 1950: "Coppi has appeared, a supernatural rider on these frightful roads used only by ancient horse-drawn carts. He wiped out these hateful roads as if invisible shock absorbers isolated him from them. Here, where for 20 years I have watched the greatest champions falter like ships on a reef and the most courageous riders lose their form and look like scissor grinders, Fausto became sublime. With a favorable wind along the last 40 kilometers, his pedal stroke seemed so airy that his wheels seemed literally to fly above the chaos of the cobbles."

It's true that the pedals, pulled powerfully along in their immutable circular path, free the cyclist's feet from all contact with the ground. This is something which until now was reserved for angels, who bring wings to the feet, and for Mercury, whose winged sandals symbolize the power of levitation and the ability to travel quickly. What a program for an aspiring champion!

But let's get back to earth and consider an analysis of cycling, this time in terms of sport ergonomics.

Seated on his saddle the cyclist doesn't fight against weight until he begins to climb. This means that on flat terrain at a slow speed he uses very little energy to move forward—barely 60 or so watts to roll at 20 kph. Half of this is used to overcome the friction caused by the movement and the other half to overcome wind resistance. If the motor hadn't been invented the bicycle would certainly have remained the vehicle *par excellence* of contemporary man, as it became again during the last war when gasoline was scarce.

Everything changes when the cyclist decides to go faster. To go from 18 kph to 25 kph he must multiply his strength by two, and by six if he wishes to reach 40 kph. At this pace he needs to pump out 400 watts. He is crossing into the domain of competitive effort. The best bicycle racers—talented experts, in good shape—reach their limit at around 600 watts and even they cannot continue at this pace for more than about an hour.

One of the great advantages of cycling is that it offers participants such a wide range of possibilities. On a bicycle you can go flat out or moderate your energy output according to your age, your motivation, and your physical abilities. There is nothing equivalent in any other sport. This idyllic picture is somewhat marred by the need to climb hills. But even this is mitigated by using tiny gears and a reasonable rate of speed to get up them efficiently. To climb a 5% grade at a walking pace a rider with a medium build uses barely 40 or so watts, and barely 100 if he wants to speed up to 10 kph. This rate is possible for most people.

Let's remember here that the watt, a unit of power, represents the work accomplished when a mass weighing 102 grams is raised vertically one meter in one second. An untrained cyclist easily has strength of around 200-250 watts at his disposal.

A second interesting and unique aspect of cycling is the *à la carte* menu it offers people at all physical levels. It can be done without sudden stresses, in a broad range of motion which calls for a gradually increasing effort from the cardiovascular system. This is useful in rehabilitating cardiac cases as well as in designing a steadily progressive training program for anyone who wants to attain good fitness. Cycling's undeniable physiological advantages come from the fact of traveling on wheels and from the great stability of the cyclist's center of gravity on the vertical plane. Because it makes use of the strongest muscles of the human body, cycling allows you to train your respiratory capacity twice as much as you could by walking or running.

Finally, because of the body position and the circular leg movement, cycling allows you to work the entire body under conditions that are radically different from those that the human organism has been accustomed to from time immemorial. Some people think of this as an inconvenience and even go so far as to speak of the sport as "unnatural." We, however, prefer to think of it as a source of new discovery and as the opportunity to experience something enriching which expands the resources and the independence of all who are tempted by, and who attempt, the great adventure that is bicycling.

equipment

Bicycles have kept the same shape since the disappearance of the highwheeler at the end of last century, when the superiority of the chain drive was established. The primary goal of this ingenious arrangement was to bring the rider closer to the ground. Until then he was dangerously perched on top of a large diameter wheel. The chain drive made the creation of the derailleur possible, some 30 years later. The simplicity and efficiency of this gearing mechanism prevails even today over more sophisticated systems.

Despite their unusual shape the so-called revolutionary bicycles are basically built just like others. They have a frame to which are attached the cyclist's static contact points (saddle and handlebars), the moving contact points (crank arms and pedals), the components for the transmission of motion (chainrings and chain), and the wheels. The rear wheel carries the freewheel cogs if it's a road bicycle or a fixed gear if it's a track bike.

In other words, a bicycle is a frame first of all. This dictates the geometry and the main mechanical characteristics. It's important to be especially careful in selecting your frame, knowing that later on and with other components you'll be able to modify your bike to different conditions, from touring to racing.

choosing a frame

We will come back to frame geometry when dealing with calculating frame dimensions in relation to the rider's build.

As one of the bike's components, the frame is characterized by its weight, its rigidity, and its mechanical qualities. The ideal frame is light and rigid. Under stress it should exhibit all the characteristics of the material from which it is built—steel, aluminum alloy, carbon fiber, fiberglass—and of the technology used to build it.

Above, the regular steel-frame professional road racing bicycle, weighing about 24 pounds.
Below, the time trial bicycle with sloping frame and disk wheels.

Weight

Ever since the invention of the bicycle, weight has been recognized as the enemy. If we take weight as the only criterion, it's clear that a heavy bicycle is tiring. This is especially true on hills but also on the flat because the rolling resistance is proportional to the weight of the man-machine unit.

Since the frame counts for approximately a fourth of the bike's total weight, the search for weight savings is justified.

The limiting factor in weight saving is the loss of rigidity that, with identical material, necessarily accompanies a reduction in frame weight. If the frame is made of steel it will be heavier or lighter depending on the use of tubing of 0.3, 0.5, 0.6, or 0.7 millimeters in thickness. The rigidity of the frame increases as a function of the tubing thickness.

For steel, the best compromise for most types of racing bicycles is achieved with 0.5 or 0.6mm tubing.

It must be noted that in descending a mountain or even a sizeable hill a heavier frame is an advantage, especially if the road conditions or uneven pavement cause a shimmy. A heavier frame increases stability and its greater rigidity provides for better bike handling at high speeds. The rider who zips down a mountain has a better feel with a somewhat heavier bike than with one that's too light.

You can shave several hundred grams off the frame weight by using aluminum alloys—whose development has been greatly advanced by adhesive bonding techniques—or, more importantly, by using carbon fiber tubing . Despite some early incidents, bikes made of these materials have passed the merciless tests of top competition, including those as demanding on equipment as Paris-Roubaix.

The weight of the frame is related to its size. Differences are marked enough for us to provide the following table, which should be used to compare different bikes independently of their components:

Material Height	50 cm	52 cm	54 cm	56 cm	58 cm	60 cm
Steel 0.7 mm	2.54	2.59	2.65	2.74	2.80	2.87
Steel 0.5 mm Reynolds 531	2.27	2.32	2.37	2.45	2.50	2.57
Steel 0.5 mm Reynolds 753	2.15	2.19	2.22	2.27	2.31	2.37
Steel 0.3 mm Reynolds 753	2.11	2.14	2.17	2.22	2.26	2.30
Duraluminum	1.63	1.67	1.71	1.75	1.79	1.83
Carbon fiber	1.59	1.63	1.67	1.70	1.74	1.78

Frame weight, including fork, in kilograms, according to P.G. Hugaud, Le Cycle.

Rigidity

It is near the joints, where mechanical stress is greatest, that a bicycle frame must have the most rigidity. This has led manufacturers to introduce tubing—called butted—that's thicker at those places.

The bottom bracket in particular is subjected to considerable stress, especially in competition when the rider stands on the pedals to start, sprint, or climb. The resulting elastic deformation of the frame is easy to demonstrate. All you need to do is push the bottom bracket sideways with your foot when the bike is held straight up with the tires inflated. You'll see that the frame flexes.

Flexing is more or less pronounced according to the material, the method of assembly, the tubing thickness, the quality of the brazing (for steel), the cross section and shape of the tubes, and the design of the lugs, if there are any.

To this day, and despite enormous progress in duraluminum and carbon fiber frames, steel frames are still the most rigid at the bottom bracket, provided the tubing is at least 0.5 mm thick.

Mechanical performance

This is a phenomenon that's difficult to explain because it's a matter of feel and depends on your style. The smooth rider who spins evenly will not have the same needs as one who tortures his bike.

The frame must be responsive to the impulses it receives and to the shocks to which it is subjected. This means that after each flexing the frame must revert to its initial shape as quickly as possible, in fractions of seconds.

In the case of steel, the quality of the tubing plays a predominant role. High performance tubing makes a clear sound when lightly flicked with the index fingernail. This is particularly true for thin tubing.

For a long time duraluminum frames were considered "mushy" because of the nature of the alloys as well as the joint assembly technique. Today's aluminum alloys are harder than their predecessors, and the adhesive bonds react better than the old mechanical joints because the adhesive transmits impulses immediately.

Carbon fiber tubing would seem to have clearly superior qualities in this area. However, for many amateurs and professionals nothing comes close to the liveliness of a steel frame provided that

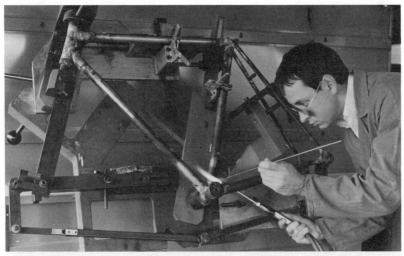

Bernard Hinault's mechanic, Alain Descroix, builds a frame. Brazing must be done under controlled temperatures. The geometry must be perfect.

the highest performance tubing on the market is used and that brazing didn't diminish its quality.

The principal advantage of a steel frame—and we will discuss this topic in another chapter—is that it permits the bike to be truly custom-fitted. This is a luxury if you're built like the standard human. But it becomes a necessity if you differ from the norm in the length of your trunk, arms, or legs—and especially the femur, the cyclist's essential lever.

choosing wheels

The so-called "700" wheel is a must for racing except for the special bikes with sloping frames and smaller front wheels that most top riders now use in time trials when the course design and profile allow. The name "700" doesn't refer to the exact wheel diameter, which actually measures between 670 and 680 mm, depending on the tire. The rim itself measures about 635 mm.

The 700 wheel used to be the trademark of a racing bike but it's now also used for leisure riding and touring. This is partly because there are now clinchers whose cross section is no greater than that of sew-ups and whose efficiency is comparable.

The 700 is especially recommended because wheel diameter is such a determining factor in frame geometry. Using this size wheel, the same frame can be used for recreation, training, or racing, according to the season or the mood of the owner. By changing a few components—for example, adding mudguards, one or two panniers, and lights—you can transform a racing bike into an acceptable touring bike.

Rims

What kind of rim should you use? How should the wheel be laced? The La Vie Claire professional team rides on four types of rims according to the race:

— 420-gram rims for normal races in the countryside, whatever the topography;

— 340-gram rims for mountain stages that include many high passes;

— 430-gram aerodynamic rims for time trials on hilly courses with long steep climbs and numerous turns. These conditions would negate the advantages of disk wheels;

— 1,600-gram disk wheels for time trials that don't require much climbing. Depending on the situation—and on the rider, who often has preferences—the mechanics put on aerodynamic rims or disk wheels. If it's windy, for example, they might only put a disk on the rear.

These numbers are valid for all riders because competition is a reliable testing ground for equipment and submits it to the toughest and longest stresses. The lightness lover is free to use narrower rims if he's confident that he can pedal smoothly and without quick starts (so he won't endanger the rear wheel) and that he can avoid potholes and stones, especially downhill. If not, beware of breakage.

Spoking

La Vie Claire team wheels are normally laced with 32 spokes, front and rear, except for cyclocross when they use 36. The spokes are triple crossed which means that each spoke crosses three others between the hub and the rim.

For time trials, aerodynamic rims are laced with 24 radial spokes in front and 28 flat spokes in the rear. Aside from aerodynamic advantages, flat spokes provide greater stiffness for the rear wheel.

Tension on the spokes must be tight. The debate on the virtues of soft wheels is over now because of the quality of our modern road surfaces.

It's also recommended to always tie the spokes in order to increase resistance to wheel deformations and to keep broken spokes in place. This also allows you to ride home without having to wait for repairs.

If you ever see a rider on Paul Köchli's team with non-tied wheels, you'll know it's due to lack of time and not to a deliberate decision by the mechanics. It's impossible to keep up with this operation routinely thoughout the season.

Tires

Manufacturers offer an extensive choice of tires according to diameter, weight, and manufacturing process.

Fausto Coppi loved to ride on 32mm sew-ups, and not just in Paris-Roubaix. He put the emphasis on comfort. Today's diameters are between 18 and 25 mm. The smaller size reduces the contact surface with the pavement and consequently the rolling resistance. We may also add that the smaller the diameter the better the aerodynamics of the wheel. This was the Wolber company's goal in producing the first 18mm sew-up for use on Renault-Gitane's Profil bike in the 1979 Tour de France.

The lighter a tire, the better it performs on the road. It's more than the weight reduction. It's the related increase in suppleness that improves the efficiency of a light tire. As long as it's properly inflated such a tire will absorb the unevenness of the road better because it returns to its cylindrical shape faster after each distortion. A heavier tire is less elastic and has greater inertia so it doesn't react as well.

The optimum tire, if you're not afraid of flats, is made of silk with an ultrathin latex innertube. Such tires are very expensive, however. They're rarely used except in track racing—even by the superchampions who used to time trial on them.

To give you an idea, the La Vie Claire team races basically all the time on 260-gram cottons with a 21.5mm diameter. For time trials they use 19mm 210-gram tires.

The sew-ups we use are hand glued. The tread is vulcanized separately and affixed to the casing which is not vulcanized. Vulcanization actually hardens the rubber and takes away some suppleness but it increases resistance to cuts and punctures.

Lesser quality sew-ups should not be ignored. They are more than adequate for training and touring, especially during the winter or in the rain, when the chance of punctures increases.

We can also mention that some sew-ups are built with a protective layer that markedly reduces the chance of puncture.

As for lightweight clinchers, they are interesting even though they haven't triumphed over sew-ups. The best ones are clearly superior to the cheapest sew-ups and may justify the purchase of a pair of clincher rims.

choosing gears

In the old days riders used to hide their fixed-gear cog from their opponents to keep their gearing secret. Some champions would go so far as to change their cog at the last minute to fool their rivals. Or they might do it because the wind had shifted enough to allow the use of a 14-tooth cog, considered a daring choice until the '50s.

Today, with two chainrings and seven-speed freewheels, the racer has so many gear ratios at his disposal that it's rare not to have the right one at his fingertips at any given moment. A triple chainring increases the possibilities further for the tourist and sometimes even for the professional. Giovanni Battaglin won the Tour of Italy in 1981 using a triple chainring in the mountain stages. However, he was the only racer we know of who dared flout common practice.

Before we examine the gears used in racing we will review some basic principles for the benefit of those who are beginning to train seriously to reach a good competitive level.

Basic principles

The word "gear" refers to a ratio. It's defined by the number of teeth on the front chainring and on the rear cog. This ratio, multiplied by the circumference of the rear wheel, gives the development or roll-out. That's the distance the bike travels with one complete crank revolution. Thus a 52x16 gear combination, a 700 rear wheel, and a tire with a 22mm cross section gives a development of 3.25 x 2.08 meters, or 6.76 meters. This takes account of not only the size of the tire but also its flattening under the rider's weight. This explains why our calculation falls quite short of the 6.94 meters usually found on gear charts. The tables use a circumference of 2.136, a value that can't be duplicated in actual conditions. With an 18mm sew-up, a gear of 52x16 gives a mere 6.70 meters.

A cyclist's gear is like a runner's stride. It's an artificial stride chosen according to the grade of the road and how hard he wants to work.

Ideally it would be nice to have a continuous changer that could select roll-outs between 2 to 10 meters with no gaps. Failing that, the derailleur lets us have 10 to 15 "speeds" on our bike depending on the number of chainrings and cogs, which isn't bad at all.

● use only good mechanical ratios

The chain's mechanical transmission of power is excellent as long as friction is minimized. This is the case when chainring and cog are precisely aligned. Power losses can be as high as 10% in cases of extreme misalignment, so it's important to avoid this.

Therefore, the smallest chainring and the smallest cog, as well as the corresponding biggest ones, should never be used together. On a seven-speed freewheel you can be even more strict and neutralize the two exterior cogs in either direction.

It's important to remember the neutralized cogs when designing gear set-ups, otherwise there will be gaps in the range.

● avoid duplication of gears

There is no advantage in obtaining almost the same gearing with two different combinations, one on the small and one on the big chainring. That's what happens, however, if you don't watch out. To deprive yourself of an additional ratio reduces the number of variations between the biggest and the smallest gear. It's in your best interest to have the most possible variations in order to give your bike the most all-round adaptability. Duplication can some-

Victory can depend on choosing the right cog. A well-stocked cog box gives you a complete range of gears.

times be overlooked in racing when the gear set-up has some other advantage. A racer rarely uses all the gears he has.

• regulate the differences between successive gears

Since continuity of muscular effort is a goal to strive for, the differences between successive gears should be as small and regular as possible. This principle favors one-tooth differences between adjacent cogs, especially in the small cogs. There the one-tooth gap becomes imperative, given the fact that the difference between 52x12 and 52x13 is 69 cm, while between 52x12 and 52x14 it's 128 cm. With the larger cogs used for mountains you have to jump two teeth and occasionally more in order to have a wide range of gears. If possible, the double-shift step from the smallest gear on the big chainring to the biggest gear on the small chainring should be the same size as the neighboring ones.

• use chainrings in sequence

To avoid a lot of switching of chainrings—which is always a little difficult, especially when climbing—it's recommended that you change only once while going through the whole range with two chainrings and only twice with a triple chainring.

• adapt the gearing to your level of training

The beginner's golden rule is not to push big gears, and to first develop good leg spin with a moderate roll-out. Even racers often spin in their 16-tooth cog while in the middle of the pack to keep their leg muscles supple and to avoid undesirable lactic acid build-up. The beginner will find it advantageous to start his freewheel with a 15, riding mostly in the 17 or perhaps the 16 after he's warmed up. The smallest cog will only be useful for short and intense efforts that will help develop muscle strength.

What chainring should you use?

A 51 or even a 50 will be sufficient for the beginner. Pros don't hesitate to start the season with a 51 for training, using their usual freewheel that begins with a 13.

If you study the development table you'll realize that it's possible to get similar gears with different chainrings. You might ask: Why not choose the 55x17 over the 52x16 as the first gear and adapt the other cogs to this combination? There are no laws against this, only customs. With the same development, bigger chainrings seem to "roll" better, meaning they are better suited to a steady effort without accelerations. For his hour record attempt in Mexico in 1984 Francesco Moser preferred the 57x15 to the 53x14, which was almost the same. But small chainrings seem to accelerate more easily. They are preferred by track sprinters who will take a 47x14 over a 54x16. This superiority of smaller chainrings in acceleration makes them better suited to the amateur who can always try bigger chainrings when he becomes more experienced. Indeed, just as they say there is always wind out on the road, there is also always a need to accelerate.

• adapt the gearing to the terrain and the type of riding

We will first deal with bikes with double chainrings.

The ordinary rider only needs two types of freewheels since he doesn't have access to a mechanic who can change the combination according to the course profile:

— one all-round freewheel;
— one freewheel for mountains.

The all-round freewheel will be adequate for almost all types of courses and will give roll-outs from approximately 3.50 to 7.50 meters. Here is an example: 52-42 with 15-16-17-18-19-21-23 will give 10 evenly spaced gears, using the first five cogs with the big chainring and the last five with the small chainring.

If you climb well, you can profitably shift to a smaller freewheel of 13-14-15-16-17-19-21. With this you can still do everything including cranking a big gear, the 52x13.

The mountain freewheel is recommended when you have to climb passes. Without wanting to be too specific in our example, a strong and well-trained rider will be able to climb a first category pass in a 42x23 without much trouble. But if the day comes when he has to climb a particularly steep grade or many passes in succession, he will find that such a gear makes him suffer too much or even forces him to get off and walk. Therefore, it's much wiser to lower the gearing a few notches. Using the same bike, you can get a 42x28 by giving up the rule of one-tooth differences between cogs sooner, as in the following example: 52-42 and 15-16-17-19-22-25-28. In this example the first four cogs are used with the big chainring and the last five with the small chainring. The one-tooth difference is maintained on the flat. Only one gear is useless—the 52x22 that duplicates the 42x17—but sometimes you have to compromise. Of course you could also deliberately sacrifice the big gears and begin with 16 teeth, using 16-17-19-21-23-26-29.

This information is good for the rider living on the flat who takes his usual double chainring bike to the mountains but changes his freewheel.

If you don't race, the best solution is a triple chainring. With a seven-speed freewheel this offers a sumptuous array of gears. Indeed, 52-40-28 and 14-15-16-17-18-20-22 offers evenly spread developments from 2.74 to 7.73 meters with 22mm tubulars, while using only good mechanical combinations (five cogs with each chainring).

Alain Descroix adjusts Bernard Hinault's bicycle

*A*ll the La Vie Claire team bicycles are maintained the same way but I have special responsibility for Bernard Hinault's bike. I've been his mechanic for the last six years. First I check that all moving parts are working properly.

Bottom bracket

I remove the crank arms in order to free the spindle so I can check the play. The axle must turn as freely as possible. I achieve this by adjusting the cup after adding some grease, but not too much. Then I tighten the lockring.

For the Grand Prix of Nations I have a special assembly technique: I install the bearings without the retainer and use motor oil instead of grease. The spindle then turns very freely and friction is reduced to a minimum. This operation requires great dexterity and I only do it in exceptional circumstances, because this assembly is more fragile and would have to be redone every day.

Hubs

I select hubs that come directly from the factory. I install them in a frame and check to see that they're not too tightly adjusted and whether they turn freely before I build the wheels.

Normally I don't adjust them but just discard those that don't satisfy me.

For the Grand Prix I remove the grease, mount them in motor oil, and adjust them for minimal play as with the bottom bracket.

Derailleur

It's very important that the derailleur pulleys be in perfect condition and that they have a minimum of play to prevent the chain from jumping, especially on seven-speed free-wheels. The problem arises with tall riders whose frames bend more at the bottom bracket shell when they're out of the saddle. The derailleur cable which passes under it then gets very stretched and the chain may jump a gear if the pulleys are not in good shape. I always replace the pulleys when I change the chain.

The axles of the derailleurs also should have very little play. Since the axles can't be adjusted I replace the derailleur if it has too much play. Or, if it's a new one, I put it aside and use another one.

The front and rear derailleur cables must be slightly slack. When needed I make sure there is a little bit of play in the shift levers. Otherwise the front derailleur cage may return poorly.

Freewheel

Occasionally freewheels don't turn as concentrically as I would like them to. They are crooked because the thread axis is off center. This can be checked visually by observing the movement of the derailleur cage. These freewheels have lateral play and oscillate vertically. I check all freewheels when they are installed with a straight edge and I only keep the best ones. If I can correct the play, however, I adjust the freewheel body with spacing rings.

We only use steel freewheels whose cogs last 5,000 km at most. Duraluminum cogs are too delicate for racers. They would rip the teeth off. As for duraluminum bodies, I never use them. When I install new cogs I often also change the chain if it's worn down too much.

Chain

The chain needs maintenance every day even in good weather. I begin by cleaning it with diesel fuel. This dislodges dirt in the links and on the axles of the chain, but doesn't degrease it too much, since it's a little greasy itself.

I then wash the bike with water and dishwashing soap, and rinse with a lot of water.

I put oil on the chain as well as on the derailleur pulleys. A chain lasts approximately 2,000 km but I change it more often in the early season because it wears out faster from the rain, which dislodges the grease and produces stiff links.

Headset

Here, too, it's important to find a good compromise between the minimum of play and a free movement of the fork on its axis.

I check the headset daily.

If the headset is pitted—that is, if it has a rough spot—I change it.

I have noticed a little-known phenomenon which deserves greater attention: Headsets are often damaged when transported on a car roof, not when the bike is in use. I came to this conclusion when I noticed that most headsets were damaged in the steering axis of the bicycle and that this even happened to bikes that had never been ridden. On a racing team we transport bikes by attaching the front fork to the car roof. This is a bad method because the headset absorbs all the road shock. But since we have to come quickly to the aid of stranded racers we have little choice to do otherwise. It would be much better to attach bikes by the saddle and handlebars.

Pedals

Here, too, I go over the bearings and grease them. After a crash I use a straight edge to check that the axles have not been bent.

Brakes

Every day I put a drop of oil behind the brake springs to prevent them from seizing.

I periodically change the brake pads, the cable housing, and the cables, especially the rear cables which have to travel farther.

Seat post and handlebar stem

I grease them to avoid seizing after every ride in the rain or at least every three months.

When the handlebars squeak because of the friction of duraluminum on duraluminum I take off the bars and grease the part that touches the stem. I do this routinely when I set up a new bike. The bars won't slip as long as you tighten the clamp properly.

Alain Descroix does
a check of the steer-
ing alignment.

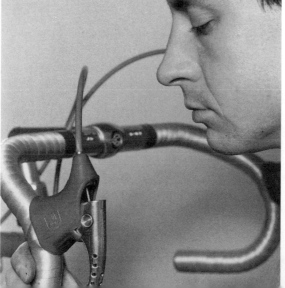

He examines the be-
ginning of the brake
cable to detect pos-
sible malfunctions.

Loosening the crank fixing bolt.

Removing the chainring.

Loosening the cogs.

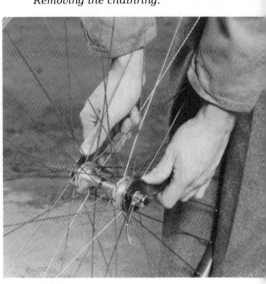

Adjusting the hub.

Loosening the handlebars.

Freeing the stem.

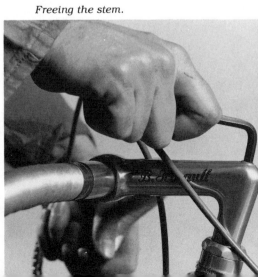

Derailleur pulleys.

Front derailleur.

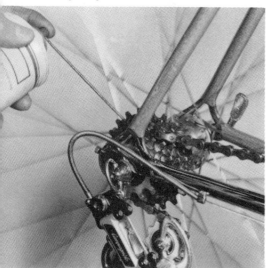

Freewheel and chain.

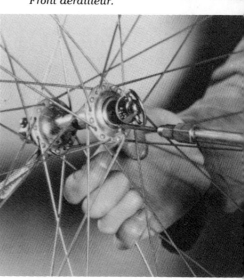

Hub.

Rear brake.

Seat post.

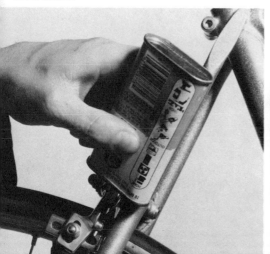

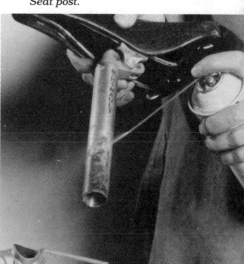

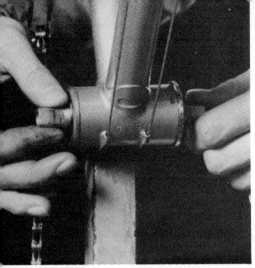

Bottom bracket axle.

Front axle.

Freewheel.

Chain tension.

Checking chain stretch.

This page: checking play.

Facing page: the final lubrication.

Wheels

Tubulars are checked every night and replaced at the smallest cut.

I take great care in wheel construction because I don't allow more than one millimeter of hop in the rim. It takes me half an hour to build a wheel. The spokes are dipped in tallow before lacing, to avoid squeaking. I file the rim on the joint to eliminate the little hump. The ferrule holes are closed with cork and I apply a layer of glue that I let dry for 24 hours. Before I mount the tire I apply another layer on the rim and on the base tape of the tire. After letting the glue dry for 10 minutes I mount the tire, taking care that the tread ribbing (if there is any) points forward on contact, so as not to lose traction in the rain or when braking.

Competition gearing

Gear choice for racing is fairly standardized after you reach a certain level of competition. All riders use the same gears—with small differences of only one or two teeth—to avoid getting dropped. So the terrain and the nature of the race are what's most important and they dictate four types of gear set-ups:
— easy course;
— very hilly course;
— mountain stage;
— time trial.

The rule of minimizing gaps between two successive gears is followed as strictly as possible.

• easy course

All the cogs are only one tooth apart, except perhaps for the biggest one. It's not a necessity, but you might want a bigger one in case of a more difficult small hill or in case you get the bonk.

Eddy Merckx liked to use a 53-44 chainring combination and a freewheel with these cogs: 13-14-15-16-17-19. With this combination, the 53x17 almost equals the 44x14, so that doesn't get used. With 42 teeth on the small chainring you could add another possibility, the 42x14. This should not be used either, however, because of the bad chain alignment. Eddy Merckx had a special fondness for the 44-tooth chainring for climbing.

Nowdays, a seven-speed freewheel lets you add a 12-tooth cog to the above set-up or put on an 18 to fill the two-tooth gap.

• very hilly course

The frequency or severity of the hills often forces you to opt for bigger cogs and, in the case of the six-speed freewheel, to eliminate the 12 tooth. In this case, with six cogs, Eddy Merckx often used 53-44 and a 13-14-15-17-19-21 freewheel.

With a seven-speed freewheel you can put a 16-tooth cog between the 15 and the 17, or add a 12. It depends on the course. A finish line on a slight downhill might persuade you to put on a 12. Very steep hills, on the other hand, will lead you to put on a 22 or 23 for your biggest cog even if that means leaving gaps between the smaller cogs. The best choice here is a 42-tooth chainring, especially in very difficult terrain, because it gives a lower gear.

• mountain stage

Usually a 23-tooth cog is adequate. It would have to be a very steep grade to make riders resort to a 24, 25 or 26. For example, a good choice might be 53-42 on the front and a 12-13-15-17-19-21-23 freewheel.

The 12-tooth cog is only kept if there is a long valley, particularly if it goes down. If not, the choice will be 13-14-15-17-19-21-23, or 13-14-16-18-20-22-24, according to the terrain.

There is no rule. The course profile will decide.

Though the rule of one-tooth differences is often ignored when it comes to big cogs, it may reappear if the average slope and the course profile allow, as in this example: 53-42 and 13-14-15-17-19-20-21. Competitors don't need as balanced a range as recreational riders because the team mechanic can figure out the necessary gears each day depending on the course.

• time trial

Because he never drafts and always goes flat out, the time trialist doesn't need a complete range of gears unless the course offers a wide variety of grades. And that doesn't happen very often. He'll try to limit shifting chainrings to save time and will put it in the big ring to go faster. In a time trial that combines flat roads and climbing he may have, for example, two cogs for the flat and four for the mountains: 53-44 chainrings and a 12-13-18-19-20-21 freewheel. Lucien van Impe once used a combination like this in the Tour de France—53-47 and 13-14-15-19-20-21—and he rode to a stage victory with it.

Fausto Coppi—shown here in the 1952 Tour de France—gave the impression of riding easily in the mountains, despite his big gears.

The six-speed freewheel is commonly used in both flat and mountainous time trials. The chain alignment is better, and the rear wheel is also slightly stronger. In a time trial the usual gearing is 53-42 and 12-13-14-15-16-17, but you can also start with a 53x13.

• gearing with a triple chainring

Professionals never use a triple chainring. But we can still discuss it for the benefit of serious cyclists or veterans who are interested in experimenting with something new.

First, here is a very classical example which has the advantage of offering good chain alignments. Each chainring is only used with four cogs of a six-speed freewheel: 52-42-35 and 12-13-14-15-16-17.

The difference between successive gears is very regular. And with the 35x17 you can practically climb trees.

The second example will be a truly original one. It resolves the problem of the great differences in development between the 12-, 13-, and 14-tooth cogs. The solution is to have a 54x13 to fill the gap between the 52x12 and the 52x13. This would put the 52 chainring at the right, the 54 in the middle, and a small 42-tooth chainring at the end. For each cog you would have two close gears by simply shifting chainrings. This arrangement is not without its advantages despite greater complexity in shifting through all the combinations. It's just a question of getting used to it.

So with 52-54-42 and 12-13-14-15-16-17-18 you would get, in succession, 52x12 (a roll-out of 9.01 meters), 54x13 (8.64 m), 52x13 (8.32 m), 54x14 (8.02 m), 52x14 (7.73 m), 54x15 (7.49 m), 52x15 (7.21 m), and 54x16 (7.02 m) for the most used gears. This represents an exceptionally well-spaced range. I propose this as an experiment and as something that goes against tradition.

The evolution of my gears

*R*obert Leroux, who introduced me to cycling, taught me *to spin my legs when I was young. Once this habit is acquired you don't forget it; it's there to stay. As an intermediate I used a 50x16 and it didn't keep me from winning races. As a junior I never went bigger than 51x14, even though there was no gear limit. I only went to a 51x13 the day of the national championships, then called "Premier Pas Dunlop," which I won in 1972.*

Nowdays I put on big gears for time trials or sprints, but only if I can afford to take them along. My big chainring usually has 53 teeth—occasionally 54 or 55, but this is rare.

In the mountains I now use smaller gears than when I was a young pro. Where I used to ride a 22-tooth cog, standing on the pedals when needed, I now use a 24 and stay in the saddle much longer. I sit further back and pedal more smoothly.

I never train with a fixed gear because I have kept the spinning ability I acquired before I was 18.

In training, at the end of winter, I put on a 51-tooth chainring and ride a lot on the 16- and 15-tooth cogs. But I quickly drop it into the 14, the 13, or even the 12. It all depends on the wind, the terrain, and the distance. In any case, you must train with all the gears used in racing as soon as good fitness comes back. I also don't like to spend a whole day in the same gear. I find it boring. Bicycling has remained a game for me, in training as well as in racing.

B.H.

special bikes

For time trial stages—just like for the pursuit on the track—almost all riders have special bikes now. As long as the course doesn't have too many turns or hills these bikes provide two kinds of advantages:

— the flywheel effect of disk wheels whose weight is greater than wheels with spokes;

— better aerodynamics than that of traditional bicycles.

The flywheel effect of disk wheels

The weight of these wheels varies greatly. In relatively flat time trials Francesco Moser uses very heavy wheels—2 kg on the front, 2.6 kg on the rear—almost identical to those he used when he set the hour record in Mexico City. This significant weight creates a flywheel effect which makes it easier to go through the dead spot and which lessens the effect of very slight decreases in output, especially for a very strong rider. However, these wheels are a real handicap as soon as there is a hill. Alain Descroix documented this by taking split times of Francesco Moser and Bernard Hinault in the 1985 Tour of Italy.

There are lighter disk wheels now, around 1.6 kg, that have even better aerodynamics and whose inertial effects are less. This allows their use in more varied terrain.

Aerodynamics

The first studies on reducing the bicycle's aerodynamic drag and improving the aerodynamics of the man-machine unit through riding position were done in 1977 by Maurice Ménard, director of the Institut Aerotechnique of Saint-Cyr-l'École and professor at the National Conservatory for Arts and Trades. From this came the Profil bicycle tested during the 1979 Tour de France and later the Delta bicycle used by Laurent Fignon in the time trial stages of the 1984 Tour de France.

Bicycles with sloping frames, cowhorn bars, and smaller front wheels had already appeared in the Eastern bloc countries. First they were used in team time trials where the purpose of the smaller wheel was to improve drafting, on the same principle as a stayer bicycle. Then, when it was realized that they had less wind resistance, they were taken to the track for the pursuit and the kilometer.

Bernard Hinault in a time trial stage of the 1985 Tour de France on his sloping bike, positioned like a skier.

It wasn't until Francesco Moser broke the world hour record in 1984 on a bicycle with a sloping frame and disk wheeels that aerodynamic studies of cyclists were taken seriously. However, aside from the wheels Francesco Moser's bike was not an aerodynamic bicycle in the strict sense of the term. The innovatively shaped frame was built with traditional round tubing without a special profile. The reduction in drag came mostly from the disk wheels and from the Italian champion's very elongated position. With the exception of the Delta bicycle almost all special bicycles now used in time trials are directly derived from Francesco Moser's bicycle. Except for the wheels, this is still very close to the first sloping-frame bicycles of the Soviets. On the flat these bicycles save 2 to 3 seconds per kilometer when compared to traditional bicycles with traditional wheels, without profiled rims or flat spokes. It's difficult to determine exactly how much should be attributed to the inertia of lenticular or disk wheels.

The current trend of research is to continue in the direction shown at Saint-Cyr-l'École in 1977. This was to reduce the drag of the bicycle itself through modifications in frame design and to create new components, such as the airplane-wing handlebars invented by Maurice Ménard in 1980 which several manufacturers copy today.

What are the limits? With the Delta bicycle the power savings had reached approximately 120 of the 200 watts a traditional bicycle consumes in wind resistance.

Although they are not as aerodynamically refined, current Moser-style bicycles offer a comparable gain thanks to disk wheels.

It's reasonable to expect to gain another 50 watts with the new generation of aerodynamic bicycles that were presented at the Milan show in 1985.

Since a superchampion can produce appoximately 600 watts in an hour, a gain of 170 watts over traditional bikes will easily put the hour record beyond 53 km at Mexico City altitudes and allow averages of 51 kph in time trials. That is if the rules, challenged once more, will allow such machines to be used.

morphology, position, and frame design

A cyclist can only achieve optimum efficiency if his bicycle is perfectly adapted to his build.

This is a problem that's much easier to state than to solve.

There are quite a few more-or-less-helpful traditional rules we will mention and whose usefulness and appropriateness we will evaluate. But primarily we'll describe the basis of a modern method. It evolved, on one hand, from current research and studies which we have both participated in and applied. On the other, it comes from our experience in top competition.

Of course we are speaking here of cycling practiced in the spirit, if not the letter, of competition, which gives the participant the will to push himself to his athletic limits. This is not the leisure riding so dear to Jean Bobet, which certainly provides other pleasures but through other means.

measuring the bicycle

A bicycle is characterized by two sets of dimensions:
— those which definitively determine its structure, no matter what accessories are put on the frame;
— those which can be changed by the choice of stem and the

Alain Descroix invented an apparatus that makes it easier to measure saddle height.

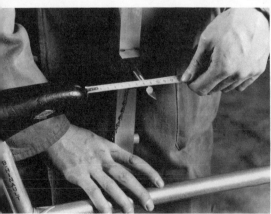

Measuring the saddle setback.

Measuring the setback of the seat tube.

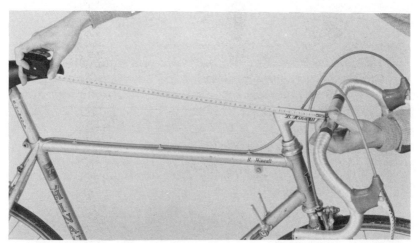

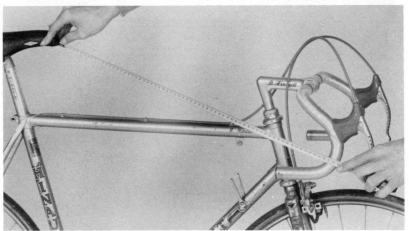

Top, measuring the saddle to handle-bar distance.

Center, measuring the distance from the saddle to the drops.

Left, checking the height of the bars from the ground.

setting of the saddle, either up and down or front and back. These are the true dimensions of position. As long as the frames are similar you must transfer these from one bike to another if you change bikes or have more than one.

Structural dimensions

Though it looks a little forbidding, it's convenient to use symbols to make the text easier to read.

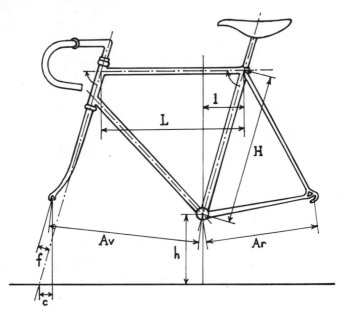

H = *frame height, center to center*
L = *frame length, center to center*
h = *height of the bottom bracket from the ground*
l = *seat tube setback*
Av = *front length, between the bottom bracket and the front wheel*
Ar = *rear length, between the bottom bracket and the rear wheel*
f = *fork rake*
c = *trail*

Measuring these dimensions takes great care and we will give more details for three of them.

● **H, frame height,** is measured parallel to the seat tube by putting the end of a ruler on the bottom bracket. Add 2 cm for the outside radius of the bottom bracket if it's steel, or 2.2 cm for most of the duraluminum ones. When in doubt, measure the shell diameter with calipers.

- l, seat tube setback, is a very important dimension which affects saddle adjustment. It's no exaggeration to say that L, the top tube length, can only be interpreted and can only make sense in conjunction with l. The meeting point of the center line of the top tube and the seat tube is easy to find. But finding the point of intersection on the top tube of a vertical from the crank axis takes more care. For this you must put the bike, with tires inflated, on a perfectly level and smooth surface. Lean it slightly to the side so that a plumb line passing directly over the crank axis almost touches the top tube. Mark this spot on the top tube. If the surface is not level turn the bike around with the wheels in the opposite places and repeat the process. Calculate from the middle of these two marks.

- f, fork rake, is difficult to measure. It's the distance between the center of the dropout and the center line of the straight part of the respective blade. You can extend the center line with a string taped just below the fork crown and measure the distance between it and the center of the dropout. It helps to have two people to measure this, to make sure the string stays on the center line of the fork and the head tube.

Dimensions of position

The dimensions of position determine the geometrical relationships between the rider's contact points—that is, the fixed points of saddle and handlebars, and the moving ones, the pedals. For the sake of simplicity the crank axle is substituted for the pedals in these calculations.

The cyclist's position is precisely calculated by the points in space of the saddle, handlebars, and crank axis in relation to a vertical, symbolizing gravity, which passes through that axis. Even though the rider is held up by his bicycle the gravity forces still act on the different parts of his body while he pedals and they contribute to his dynamic equilibrium.

There are other ways of measuring position which are well worth considering. But we have chosen this one because it's easy to measure on a traditional bike.

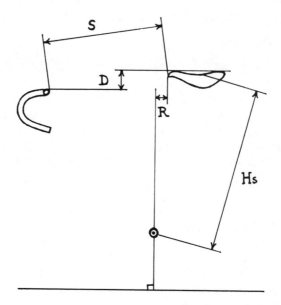

Hs = *saddle height, the distance between the bottom bracket and the deepest part of the saddle.*

R = *saddle setback, the distance between the nose of the saddle and a vertical to the bottom bracket.*

S = *saddle to handlebar distance, between the nose of the saddle and the horizontal part of the bars where they meet the stem.*

D = *saddle-stem distance, the difference in height between the saddle and the stem at their highest point above the frame.*

● **Hs, saddle height,** is measured by putting a carpenter's square horizontally on the saddle so that its longest side is at the lowest point of the saddle. As you did for the frame height, measure the distance from the bottom bracket to the edge of the square, adding a similar amount for the radius of the shell.

● **R, saddle setback,** is very easily measured once the vertical from the crank axis has been marked on the top tube. Place the square horizontally along the tube and vertically against the nose of the saddle.

● **S, saddle-handlebar distance,** is measured by putting a yard-stick with one end touching the handlebar tube next to the stem and the other resting on the nose of the saddle. The slope of the measuring stick, which results from the difference in height between the stem and the saddle, does not present any major problems. You could calculate or measure this horizontally, but that seems like a useless refinement.

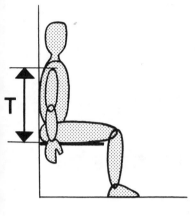

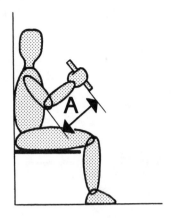

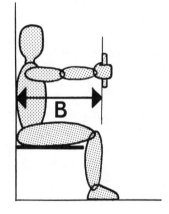

Measuring the rider

These simple body dimensions are enough.
- *Above left, the trunk T.*
- *Above right, the forearm A.*
- *Facing, the arm B.*
- *Below left, the thigh C.*
- *Below right, the lower leg J.*

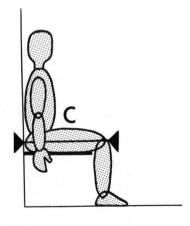

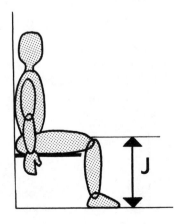

- **D, saddle-stem height,** is easily obtainable from the difference between the top of the stem and the top of the saddle nose relative to the top tube.

measuring the cyclist

With seven body measurements that are easy to take and don't require any special anatomical knowledge it's possible to make an anthropometric description of a person which is perfectly adequate to use for reliable data on the dimensions of a rider's optimum position. From this you can also experimentally deduce the dimensions of his bicycle.

- **height:** everyone knows his or her height, which is indicative when used with other dimensions but is notoriously insufficient when used as the only morphological criterion.

- **inseam E:** this is the most important dimension to know—that's not surprising when it comes to cycling. We measure the inseam with a big carpenter's square about 1.5cm wide whose long side is set against a wall. The racer must be in riding shorts, without shoes, and with feet slightly spread. Raise the square as much as possible and mark the maximum height on the wall.

- **thigh C:** the rider sits on a stool, with his back straight and his pelvis flat against the wall. Lower legs must be vertical. Put a straight edge against the two kneecaps and measure the distance from there to the wall.

- **lower leg J:** in the same position as for the thigh, without shoes, but this time you put the straight edge on top of the knees in front of the beginning of the thigh muscles, making sure to keep the lower legs vertical. Measure the distance from the straight edge to the ground.

- **trunk T:** sitting on a stool whose top must be level the rider presses pelvis and back against the wall, keeping the shoulders horizontal. Place the square on the bulge of the collarbone and measure the distance between the mark on the wall at this height and the top of the stool.

• **arm B:** keeping his previous position, the rider lowers his arm and grabs a small cylinder the same diameter as the handlebars. A small aspirin jar or something similar is fine. Without moving the shoulders forward and with the back against the wall, the subject moves his straight arm to a horizontal position. Measure from the wall to the edge of the cylinder.

• **forearm A:** with the arm at 45 degrees, the rider bends his elbow at a right angle, making sure that the cylinder in his hand stays perpendicular to his forearm. Measure the distance between the point of the elbow and the cylinder.

optimum position and bike dimensions

Most of the builders who make so-called custom bikes use simplified sizing methods. Some estimate the frame height from charts based on the rider's height. Others have the rider mount a bike or an adjustable contraption like a home trainer and make their decision based on how the rider looks while pedaling.

The drawbacks of this last method are that the rider is not really exerting himself and that appearances are not always enough, even when supported by experience.

The problem actually breaks down into several:

— what position will give the rider maximum efficiency, reducing physical effort while maintaining his performance level?

— what frame dimensions will allow him to adopt this position? Even though a bicycle is adjustable, it's only within rather narrow parameters. It may be impossible to set the saddle back as far as you want on a bike whose seat tube is too vertical. And if the frame is much too small it's impossible to put the handlebars at the right distance, except with an oversized stem that will compromise the riding and aesthetic qualities of the bicycle;

— what frame geometry will make the bicycle a good locomotive vehicle, holding the road, stable at high speed, and turning easily? This mostly depends on the length of the front end, the fork rake, the trail, and the angle of the head tube with the top tube.

Strictly speaking, these three questions must be answered in succession in the order given above. This also explains why it's practically impossible for a beginner to get a perfectly fitting custom bike on the first try. Even pros slowly modify their bike dimensions. At least the best ones do, perfecting their style and position as they gain more experience. But this doesn't keep them from winning races at the beginning of their careers, even on an imperfect bike. For though it's important to take this seriously, as it deserves, it is also counterproductive to become a fanatical perfectionist. As Paul Wiégant, former coach of the A.C.B.B., used to say, "It takes more than bike dimensions to make a rider."

Bernard Hinault's bicycles, or, the short history of a position

*I*t was in 1978 during the Tour de France that I began to systematically measure pro riders' bicycles, to collect the data needed for studies of riding position. Here is the design of the bike Bernard Hinault was riding then:

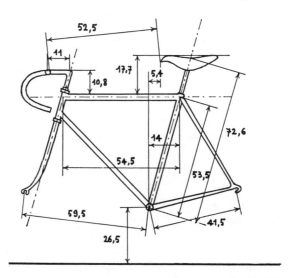

The following year near the end of January Bernard Hinault rode the French national cyclocross championships on

his way to race in the Rotterdam six-day. At that time I measured his cyclocross and his track bike, so I could make some comparisons. On that occasion I noticed that the saddle of his road bike, which he had brought along, was pushed all the way back. This meant that Bernard still hadn't been able to find his definitive position, since his frame geometry wouldn't allow him to set the saddle further back. I mentioned this to Cyrille Guimard, then his directeur sportif, and he later told me that a new frame was being studied, as a result of ergonometric research and wind tunnel tests done at the Renault company.

It took Bernard Hinault many months to get used to his new position, whose remarkable efficiency confirmed the studies completely. But the saddle wasn't immediately set at the desired height—there were still several millimeters to go. It was with this bike, slanted back much more, that the Breton won the Criterium of the Dauphiné Libéré for the second time, by almost 13 minutes, and the Tour de France, in which he masterfully took seven stages, including the last two.

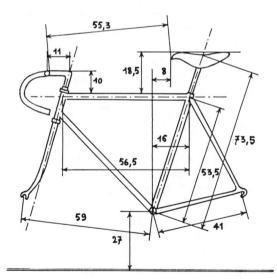

We note in passing that the two most widely accepted empirical methods of calculating frame height give dimensions which are far from reality:

— if you subtract 25 cm from Bernard Hinault's 83cm inseam you get 58 cm which is really a long way off;

— *if you use the usual printed chart that gives the frame height according to the rider's height you get 56 cm which is hardly any better. Bernard Hinault is 1.73 meters tall, and these tables give a frame height of 55 to 57 cm for a person 1.70 to 1.75 m.*

From 1979 to 1982 his saddle height was carefully and gradually raised from 72.8 to 73.5 cm, following the recommendations of the ergonometricians.

The year 1983 was marked by the knee operation, after a mistake in setting his saddle during the Tour of Spain (which he won anyway). This mistake—which was the final provocation, if not the actual cause—forced Bernard Hinault to pedal on a saddle raised to 74 cm for the whole long mountain stage in which he assured his final victory. A sudden increase of 5 mm—especially in such a difficult stage—couldn't help but damage the tendons of a rider whose position was being adjusted so precisely and gradually. If the saddle had been lowered instead of raised it wouldn't have done the same thing. A saddle that's too low reduces efficiency but it doesn't cause this kind of injury.

When Bernard Hinault got back on his bike after his operation during the summer of 1983 he started with a saddle height of 72 cm, so as not to make too strenuous a demand on his knee tendons. He raised his saddle very slowly. On November 11, 1983, at a cyclocross in Brouilly he was still only at 72.5 cm.

He started the '84 Tour de France at 72.9 cm and ended it at 73.2 cm.

He finished his great '84 season with a saddle height of 73.4, winning the Grand Prix of Nations and the Tour of Lombardy in rapid succession. When he started the '85 season he had reached his optimum height—73.5cm—and he hasn't changed it since.

At the end of 1983 Bernard Hinault left Renault to help Bernard Tapie start the La Vie Claire team, and his personal mechanic Alain Descroix joined him in this venture. The bike he had constructed then was practically the same as the one he had been using. At the most you could see a slight increase in the frame height and a greater setback of the seat tube—5 mm for each measurement. The riding position is practically identical, with slightly more setback of the saddle and a slightly lower stem for aerodynamics.

C.G.

Above, Bernard Hinault's former position, shown in the 1978 Grand Prix of Nations, which he won. The more you pedal seated forward the more likely you are to move to the nose of the saddle when you go hard.

At right, Bernard Hinault's new position, the balance and stability of which are apparent here on the Champs-Élysées in Paris at the finish of the 1979 Tour de France.

Calculating position measurements

Eddy Merckx, a perfectionist in mechanical things if there ever was one, used to change his saddle height during races with a key he always carried in his jersey pocket. This did not escape the notice of race observers.

What is less well known is that he only did this because of what happened to his lower vertebrae in a terrible accident in which his trainer Georges Wambst died. It was a nighttime derny race at the Blois velodrome and the lights went out suddenly. This was in 1969 after his first victory in the Tour de France, and one can only imagine the triumphs he would have achieved if he had not been handicapped by this accident from then on.

Eddy Merckx didn't change his saddle height to adapt his position to the type of effort required, as was believed, but quite simply to alleviate his back pains. The Belgian superstar believes that one always should keep the same riding position, and it took him five years to perfect his.

With the help of ergonomics and mathematical studies on optimum position it's now possible to proceed more quickly.

Here are the main results of those studies:

● the sequence of adjustments

The saddle absolutely must be adjusted first. The saddle is the main contact point. Its position relative to the cranks will determine the ergonomic conditions of the movement of the tie rods (in cycling jargon) which are the legs.

The handlebars come next. They must be set up in such a way that the cyclist can take turns riding with his hands on the drops at speed or more upright with his hands on the tops the rest of the time.

It's impossible to compensate for a bad saddle adjustment by playing with the position of the bars, which can vary with the type of race.

For example, when Francesco Moser set the world hour record in Mexico in 1984 he rode a bicycle whose saddle height and setback were adjusted exactly like his road bikes. But his cowhorn bars were set up to bring his hands 5 centimeters further forward. We think, however, that this great difference forced him to ride more on the nose of the saddle than he would have liked.

● saddle height Hs

This is a very important dimension which can be calculated to within a few millimeters by using a mathematical formula.

The contrast between these two positions is dramatic. Roger de Vlaeminck, below near the end of Paris-Roubaix, appears very much at ease on his bike. His flat back helps aerodynamics and opens the rib cage. His arms, bent at a right angle, allow easy breathing and work well as shock absorbers.

On the other hand, Luis Ocana, above in the 1973 Tour de France prologue, strains to pedal seated at the tip of a saddle which is too high and too far forward. The bars are too close, forcing him to round his back, contract his shoulders, and stiffen his arms. It's very helpful to develop a supple body if you want to achieve a good riding position.

With cambered shoes, the saddle height Hs can be calculated from a given inseam E with the following formula:

$$Hs = 0.885 \times E$$

The saddle height derived from this formula represents the optimum one for a road rider and suits modern cycling, which combines power and suppleness. In most cases it gives the greatest efficiency for the effort.

In the past—and even today for many who have not had the benefit of studies similar to those made by the Renault company's physiology and biomechanics laboratory—bicycle racers used to sit lower. Traditional empirical methods do not generally lead to raising the saddle this high either. When Laurent Fignon joined the Renault-Gitane team, his saddle was raised 1.5 cm. We could go on with examples.

If you start with a position much lower than that indicated, it's important to raise the saddle little by little over several months so that muscles and tendons become gradually accustomed to it.

Your feelings must be your guide. It's better not to force yourself to adopt some particular saddle height if the resulting position doesn't have the right feel. But keep in mind that the body can be retrained, even if a habit is second nature. The foot's range of motion allows you to adjust your pedaling, even if it seems strange at first.

Having said this, let's not forget that no rule should be blindly followed. The numbers propose, the rider disposes.

• saddle setback R

Ergonomics teaches us that for road riding it's more efficient to pedal "at the back," with a sizeable setback of the saddle, rather than "at the front." There are two main reasons for this:

— it's easier to push your foot forward when crossing the upper dead spot and to pull it back at the lower dead spot. This has the effect of smoothing out the pedal stroke by increasing the continuity of the force exerted on the pedals.

— pushing with the foot tends to stabilize the pelvis on the saddle. This also evens out the stroke, since the legs can then be used solely for propulsion without getting involved, as a reflex, in counteracting the natural tendency to slide forward on the saddle when the effort is intense.

The more forward the saddle, the more the rider will slide forward because of a shift at the lower end of the power zone portion of the stroke.

However, it's difficult for some riders to adopt such a position because they lack suppleness and lower back strength.

What we will give here will be a direction to follow rather than a rule in the proper sense of the word. Note that appropriate back and hamstring stretching exercises will significantly increase suppleness, especially if you start young. A table below gives ranges of saddle setback according to inseam.

• saddle-handlebar distance S

Once the saddle is correctly adjusted you have to put the handlebars the right distance from the tip of the saddle so you'll be comfortable on the drops and also when riding upright with your hands on the tops. The margin of choice is fairly large. Though it can be catastrophic to race a whole stage on a saddle which is suddenly raised by a few millimeters—especially if it's already at its maximum—the saddle-handlebar distance can easily be increased half a centimeter, or even a full centimeter for a time trial.

The longer your trunk, arms, and forearms the more you can increase the distance beween saddle and bars, obviously.

These are not the only factors to consider. It's so much easier to stretch out on a bike whose saddle is adjusted according to criteria of biomechanical efficiency—that is, high and back enough. That's because it's easier for the chest to lean forward in this position than when you sit too low and on the nose of the saddle.

Aside from its aerodynamic advantage, this position allows you to push the bars with your arms. This decreases the work of the lower back muscles while promoting the stability of the pelvis on the saddle.

We won't provide strict rules to calculate the saddle-handlebar distance but only approximate ranges, just as we did for the saddle setback.

• saddle-stem difference D

Old treatises recommended you set your stem barely lower than the saddle because at that time road riders sat on their bicycles with their chests more upright than nowadays. With a modern position it's essential to lower the stem by quite a few centimeters to improve aerodynamics. Francesco Moser doesn't hesitate to set his stem 10 cm below the saddle.

• summary table

This table is not really binding.
It only indicates ranges of value for three dimensions—saddle setback R, saddle-handlebar distance S, and saddle-stem difference D—as a function of the inseam E and for a normally proportioned body.

Our preference would be for the larger dimensions, except in particular cases. These dimensions can even be exceeded if the femur (for the saddle setback) or the trunk, arm, and forearm (for the other two dimensions) are proportionally longer than average. Contrary to common belief, the posture "pelvis fairly high and toward the back, head down, and back stretched" is best for a good spine position. It's also the most efficient.

E	R	S	D
75 to 78 cm	4 to 6 cm	47 to 41 cm	5 to 6 cm
79 to 82 cm	5 to 7 cm	50 to 54 cm	6 to 7 cm
83 to 86 cm	6 to 8 cm	53 to 57 cm	7 to 8 cm
87 to 90 cm	7 to 9 cm	56 to 60 cm	8 to 9 cm

• morphological differences

When you start looking for your optimal position you have to know your morphological peculiarities in order to adjust the data given in the table above in the right direction. Divergence from the average build can change the numbers quite a bit.

The femur. The cyclist's lever, the femur can be longer or shorter relative to the tibia in different people.

The norm in the ratio of the thigh C to the lower leg J (as we defined them) is an average of 1.11 in men. But it's a more favorable 1.14 in women, who are thereby blessed by nature. And to think that some people are against the development of women's bicycle racing!

A clearly larger ratio between these segments of the leg has been observed in several very great champions such as Fausto Coppi (1.18), Eddy Merckx (1.16), and Bernard Hinault (1.20) whom we dare to mention here in the third person. Climbing abilities are improved. We may wonder if Francesco Moser is not handicapped in this area of cycling by the length of his tibia (a ratio of 1.10), despite his very great athletic talent.

If the ratio C/J is well above 1.11 you can try setting the saddle further back.

If, on the contrary, the tibia predominates it would perhaps be better to raise the saddle somewhat.

On the top of the bars near the stem.

On top of bars with arms more spread out.

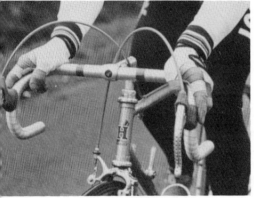
Closer to the brake hoods.

Hands below on the drops.

With his hands on the brake hoods, Bernard Hinault keeps his fingers relaxed.

When going hard, the hands grip the drops.

The trunk and the arms. A longer trunk or longer arms (especially the forearms when in a horizontal position gripping the drops) will lead you to increase the distance between the saddle and the handlebars. This will have an effect on the length of the frame and the stem. To know this you only need to calculate the ratio of the trunk T, the arm B, and the forearm A over the inseam E.

Normally: $T/E = 0.76$ $B/E = 0.87$ $A/E = 0.40$

If your ratios are larger you are in the same situation as the example given in the previous paragraph.

Pro racer Pascal Jules has a frame whose top tube is 58.5 cm and center to center height is 53.3 cm, an unusual geometry far from the square frame.

Why?

Because he has a very long trunk and long arms, as the following ratios show when compared to the average:

— $T/E = 0.86$, trunk longer by 8 cm;
— $B/E = 0.93$, arms longer by 5 cm;
— $A/E = 0.45$, forearms longer by 4 cm.

Differences like that, confirmed by a concrete example, show the advantage of this method.

We don't use the ratio of the inseam to the height (which generally is 0.47) because the size of the head and neck, which have nothing to do with position, falsify the results.

The traditional
ways
of setting position

*U*ntil the appearance of methods based on body measurements a cyclist depended on three elementary rules to set up his position on the bike.

Heel on the pedal

"The saddle height should allow you to pedal without shifting from side to side when you put the heels of the shoes on the pedals."

This rule, which dates from the time when the soles were flat, prevents any major errors. It's much less valuable since sport cyclists began using strongly arched shoes that naturally put the foot in an extended position to help in the pulling up phase and in spinning.

We see, moreover, that a too-pronounced hip shifting (how can this be defined, with a simple rule?) doesn't necessarily prove the saddle is too high. It can result from a lack of decontraction of the opposing muscles while pedaling and from a lack of suppleness in ankle movement, all things which can be corrected by a well-rounded training program. Style is also involved, according to whether you pedal with your toes or your heels down.

This method usually leads to a saddle height which is too low, which doesn't assure the optimum efficiency but loses power and counteracts the correct working of the hamstring muscles, especially on climbs.

Plumb line from the kneecap

It was Daniel Clément, former French national cycling coach, who was the first to look for a method of determining the saddle setback by taking the sections of the leg into account.

"Sit on the saddle in a normal position, shoes in the toeclips, with the cranks horizontal and the bike on a perfectly level surface. A plumb line which passes from the end of the femur of the forward leg, just behind the hollow of the kneecap, should basically fall over the pedal axle."

This method helps avoid riding seated too far forward. But it's limited by the fact that the rider is stationary and not in a working condition. It may be that you can set your saddle back even more. That was the case with Bernard Hinault. Robert Leroux had used the plumb line rule on him but the ergonometric studies later improved on this by setting his saddle back several centimeters in 1979.

Brushing the elbow and knee

To set up the distance from the saddle to the bars, some recommend bending the arms to a right angle, hands on the tops, and making sure the knee brushes the elbow when the leg comes up while pedaling.

This method is not convincing. First, the concept of brushing is very fuzzy. Also, it would mean that a rider whose torso is abnormally long would have to fold himself up to follow the rule. This is without theoretical foundation and, beyond that, is contrary to the need to stretch the spinal *column to the maximum to avoid a rounded back.*

It's better to rely on the norms we indicated. Adjust them if necessary according to the relative length of the trunk, the arms, and the forearms. Above all, look for the right feel in learning to push on the bars when riding in an aerodynamic position with your chest horizontal.

C.G.

Determining the bicycle dimensions

As a pedaling machine the bicycle is principally characterized by three structural dimemensions:
— the frame height, center to center, H
— the setback of the seat tube, l
— the top tube length, center to center, L

As we will see, the frame height is calculated very easily as a function of the inseam.

The setback of the seat tube l and the frame length L are determined graphically, independently of each other (this point is very important) from the position measurements, once these have been determined.

• calculating the frame height H

If there is a dimension which can be arrived at mathematically within a half centimeter of accuracy it is frame height.

Indeed:

— the saddle height, for all purposes proportional to the inseam, strictly depends on the length of the lower limbs and to a lesser extent on the proportions of their segments;

— the frame height is proportional to the saddle height because of the frame structure and because of the need to have enough seat post showing so that the handlebar stem can be low enough to satisfy aerodynamic needs.

It follows that the frame height depends only on the leg length.

Consequently, the tables that give frame height as a function of the rider's height are inadequate. We have had many occasions to verify this fact.

— Reproduced year after year from book to pamphlet, these tables lead to choosing a frame that is always too big, even for people with average build. The pro racers we measured had an average height of 1.77 m and an inseam of 84 cm and their average frame height was close to 55.5 cm. However, the tables we mentioned recommend that riders between 1.75 and 1.80 m use a frame between 57 and 58 cm, or an average of 2 cm too much. This is a very significant difference.

— These tables don't take morphological disparities (short or long trunk) into account and so they introduce a new source of error.

Another equally well-known rule also gives false results: The center-to-center frame height is obtained by subtracting 25 cm from the inseam. If we apply this rule to Lucien van Impe, a small rider, we arrive at a frame size of 53.5 cm, whereas he finds a 50cm frame sufficient. For Dietrich Thurau, who is very big, it gives 66 cm but he is comfortable with a 59cm frame. As we can see, this method leads to major errors whose cause is twofold:

— a rule based on a simple subtraction and not on proportionality is necessarily inaccurate and leads to recommending unusually tall frames for big riders;

— the rule comes from a time when frames, even for racing, were bigger than those used today. The aerodynamic position with flattened trunk had not yet been adopted by road racers but was a trademark of track riders.

To calculate the center-to-center frame height precisely you merely have to multiply the inseam E by 0.65.

This coefficient can be raised to 0.66 for tourists who don't need to lower their stem for aerodynamics.

The validity of our coefficient was confirmed recently by a former mechanic of Eddy Merckx. He figured frame height using the distance between the ground and the top of the kneecap of the seated rider. It happens that this body dimension (lower leg J, as we called it) is precisely equal to 0.65 times the inseam according to our anthropometric statistics.

• setback of the seat tube l

This dimension is fundamental to frame geometry because it dictates the seat tube angle. If the setback of the seat tube is insufficient it may be impossible to push the saddle far enough back to achieve the desired position.

A frame is well designed when the continuation of the seat tube crosses the saddle at its lowest part, which usually coincides with its middle.

The drawing below illustrates the different steps to follow:

— draw two circles from the center of the bottom bracket. The first radius, H, corresponds to the frame height and the second radius, Hs, to the saddle height;

— draw a vertical line passing through the center of the bottom bracket;

— draw a parallel behind this vertical line at the distance "saddle setback plus half the saddle length";

— determine the meeting point of this line with the big circle and join this point to the center of the bottom bracket;

— the line that joins the center of the bottom bracket to the middle of the saddle intersects the small circle at the axes of the meeting point of the seat tube and top tube. We now can measure l.

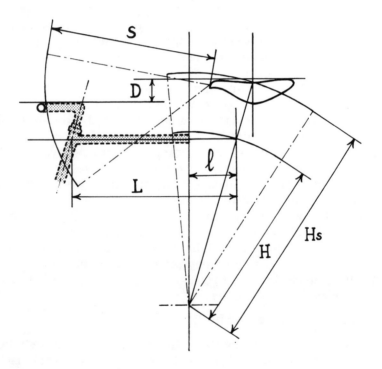

• frame length L

The distance between the saddle and the bars can be the same with different frame lengths because you can play with the stem length.

This leeway allows you to find the right position on almost any bicycle with acceptable dimensions.

The drawing shows how you can simultaneously calculate the top tube and stem length once the saddle-handlebar distance S and the saddle-stem difference D is known.

— draw the saddle and the seat post, as in the previous diagram;

— draw a circle whose center is the nose of the saddle with the radius S;

— draw a horizontal line at the distance D from the line marking the top of the saddle;

— the diameter of the handlebars is a little circle tangent to this line and to the circle;

— draw the stem to a predetermined size and draw the axis of the head tube which will meet the axis of the top tube at the point we are looking for.

The length L we got this way can be increased, at least in theory, by 1 or 2 cm if you shorten the stem length by the same amount.

In practice, you have to make a choice.

By what criteria should this choice be made?

This is where you have to consider the riding qualities of the bicycle, looking at it no longer as a pedaling machine but as a means of locomotion. These qualities—stability on descents, road-holding, turning behavior—depend on the design of the front of the bicycle. That is, they depend on the head tube angle, the front length, the fork rake, and the trail, which are all interdependent.

The frame builder's art consists in choosing these dimensions well. We'll content ourselves with only a few general comments on the topic:

— the front length depends on the rider's size. It will be 60 or even 61 cm on a big rider but will not go much below 58 on a road bike for a small rider. The problem is stability, especially on descents. You shouldn't worry if your foot hits the front wheel when you turn the handlebars unless you like doing a trackstand at red lights, in which case you increase your chance of falling;

— the trail should be between 4.5 and 6 cm for a front end that is both stable and maneuverable;

— the head tube should not have too big a slope nor be too upright but have an angle between 72 and 74.5 degrees in most cases.

For those who love norms, here is a table which provides purposely approximate ranges of stem length as a function of frame length.

Frame length	Stem
46 cm	8 to 10 cm
48 cm	9 to 11 cm
50 cm	9.5 to 11.5 cm
52 cm	10 to 12 cm
54 cm	10.5 to 13 cm
56 cm	11 to 13.5 cm
58 cm	11.5 to 14 cm
60 cm	12 to 14 cm

Today's trend is to have longer stems than before because bicycles are more compact. This puts greater weight on the front wheel—a plus for stability—and makes the front end more maneuverable.

The patient search for definitive dimensions

The beginning rider will not find his ideal position overnight. Many years are often needed to achieve perfection to within a few millimeters. Trial and error takes time and, above all, the body changes little by little. With training it acquires new abilities. Agility increases, muscles become stronger, skills improve. In short, the walker becomes a rider and integrates the bicycle as an extension of himself.

This is why the numbers we give for the dimensions of position contain a margin for personal taste and must be used as a guide, as a direction for experimentation. For example, a big rider whose saddle setback is only 5 cm, or whose saddle is 2 cm too low (when compared to our figures) would find it in his interest to slowly and systematically try a set-up that conforms more to the typical optimum position.

Understanding the static and dynamic functioning of your body is an invaluable aid in this situation. If you push on the bars with chest down, forearms level, and elbows bent at an obtuse angle it's easier to see the advantages of a saddle that is high enough and set back far enough than when you are content to sit on the bike passively, turning the cranks by habit.

The search for the right "feel" absolutely must go along with setting up your position. The blind application of norms and coefficients is not enough. The mathematics of living beings cannot be brought down to the level of general mechanics.

Anthropological norms must be taken in the same spirit—that is, without giving undue importance to the numbers.

The coefficients we provide make it possible, above all, to evaluate significant differences. The example of Pascal Jules clearly illustrates this and indicates the steps to take. If you discover through some quick calculations that you have a build like his you'll avoid trying to find a good position on a regular bike whose frame will be too short.

In conclusion, here is the complete order to follow:

— establish your morphological data, noting significant differences;

— calculate the frame height and saddle height from your inseam. These two dimensions can be precisely determined from the coefficients we gave;

— evaluate the range of the other dimensions of position with the help of the table, but adapt them to the morphological data;

— ride for a while on a bike compatible with these new position dimensions until you discover the best set-up. Special attention should be given to the setback of the seat tube. If this doesn't allow a correct saddle position—and this is the case with bikes whose seat tube is too upright—there is no need to continue because the undertaking is doomed. This phase of perfecting can last several months, depending on physical abilities and on your eagerness to train;

— finally, have a truly custom bicycle built, perfectly adapted to you, like the pros whose machines are defined to the millimeter. This will be the reward for your efforts.

choosing cranks

Crank length is the subject of great controversy in cycling circles, like big gears used to be a few years ago.

Should you or shouldn't you adapt your crank length to your leg length?

So stated, the question is clear and if you follow common sense it calls for a yes answer.

Yet the pros almost exclusively use 170 to 175mm cranks—a 3% variation—whereas their inseams may vary from 72 cm (Jean Robic) to 91 cm (Eddy Merckx). There's a difference of 26% between these extremes.

The most widespread opinion is that a rider shouldn't increase his crank length for fear of injuring his ligaments, because longer cranks increase the angles between the segments of the leg when pedaling. If the change occurs brutally without adjusting position and without progressive adaptation there may indeed be a risk. But in absolute terms the hypothesis is unfounded because the range of motion was smaller when Eddy Merckx used 175mm cranks than when Jean Robic rode with 170mm ones. And Jean Robic never experienced any problems with his ligaments. To ride like Jean Robic, Eddy Merckx would have needed 210mm cranks. This analysis was proven correct by the Renault company's physiology and biomechanics laboratory. Tall riders using 175mm cranks submitted their legs to smaller angular variation than smaller riders using 170mm cranks. Without going into the details of the biomechanical arguments we can say that a cyclist who spins at the same speed in the same gear with longer cranks will decrease the force he must exert on the pedals. Consequently he will save some muscular energy. This energy can be kept for the end of the race or to ride faster if he feels like it. For example, with 180mm cranks in a 52x13 gear the muscular effort, especially in the zone of power, is practically the same as with 170mm cranks and a 52x14. This advantage explains why Jacques Anquetil, the best big-gear specialist of his day, used 180mm cranks for the Grand Prix of Nations whereas his usual cranks measured only 175 mm. For the same reason, André Darrigade used to switch from 170 to 175 mm for the high passes of the Tour de France, Eddy Merckx from 175 to 177.5 mm in the mountains and in time trials, and Roger Rivière from 172.5 to 175 mm in his successful attempts at the world hour record, even on the track where you have to spin.

Jean Robic used very long cranks for his height. This gave him a great advantage, especially in the mountains. To keep the same proportions Eddy Merckx would have had to use 210 mm cranks to get the same leg angles when pedaling.

To temporarily mount longer cranks for the mountains or time trials is a well-established practice, even if not everyone does it, like Francesco Moser and Bernard Hinault.

The question is whether you should routinely use long cranks if you're tall.

In the peloton you mostly only find three sizes: 170, 172.5 and 175 mm.

If you want to be like the pros, most of whom believe that you don't spin as well beyond 175 mm even if you're tall, you can adopt the following length according to your inseam:

— from 74 to 80 cm: 170 mm;
— from 81 to 86 cm: 172.5 mm;
— from 87 to 93 cm: 175 mm.

This shouldn't keep you from further increasing these sizes by 2.5 or even 5 mm for an uphill race, a time trial, or in the mountains, if you're careful during training to adjust to a slightly different saddle position to keep your feeling of optimum efficiency.

If you're more daring and want to experiment with new solutions, you may safely try longer cranks according to your inseam:

— from 74 to 77 cm: 170 mm;

— from 78 to 81 cm: 172.5 mm;
— from 82 to 85 cm: 175 mm;
— from 86 to 89 cm: 177.5 mm;
— from 90 to 93 cm: 180 mm.

You may be interested to learn that the 1985 winner of Paris-Roubaix, Marc Madiot, has an inseam of 86 cm but rides year-round with 180mm cranks in training as well as competition. This should quiet any worry about possible risks to the ligaments.

Jacques Anquetil's cranks

U nlike certain champions Bernard Hinault has always been very cautious about his cranks and never changed them even in the mountains, even in time trials. Always 172.5 mm.

I can share his feelings on one point: if you want to make the most of cranks of any length it's better not to change them, but keep the same ones.

On the other hand I'm convinced that riders are being timid when they stubbornly spin 175mm cranks when they have a 90cm inseam, and that they would improve their performance without changing their style by permanently switching to 180 mm. That's the only way to get your legs used to these levers.

Jacques Anquetil gave me some very interesting information about this:

"When I started I used 170 mm like everybody else. Certain that I would benefit by using longer cranks I very soon went on to 172.5 mm. It was in 1959 that I made the decisive jump to 175, which at that time was considered a very long crank. At 1.76 m I'm not a tall guy but I was convinced I went faster with the 175s and I couldn't see any reason to give them up. I had tested them in time trials with success. At first I used them in training a little before the race. That gave me slight back pains so I eventually preferred to put them on only the day of the race. That was where I needed the most benefit, though it increased the risk of having sore legs the next day. When I decided to use 175 all the time it took me a year to truly get used to it. But I persisted and I was right—the results proved it. After that

The best time trial stylist, Jacques Anquetil, used 177.5mm cranks and even 180 mm in the Grand Prix of Nations, which he won 9 times.

I was able to use 177.5 and even 180 mm in time trials and in mountain stages."

Jacques Anquetil's inseam is 84 cm, so his 175 mm corresponds to the second table in the section about choosing cranks.

They often say that a young rider, even if he's tall, should use 170 mm because he doesn't need big gears. I think exactly the opposite. It's when you're young that you acquire the technique of pedaling, repeated hundreds of thousands of times. Therefore you should use the cranks that are best for your height from the start of your career and spin as if it were nothing. With a 90cm inseam and 180mm cranks you're still a long way from the threshold of articular incompatibility that would definitely come beyond 210 mm. The question of gears has nothing to do with it. The point is to learn to spin. When you get old enough to use bigger gears it's worth another whole tooth. This is my personal point of view and only mine.

C.G.

cleat adjustment

Fixed to the sole, the cleat binds the cycling shoe to the pedal. Without this accessory—or a similar contraption that has the same function, such as the Look system—it's impossible to pedal at peak efficiency. This is because, first, a moving foot doesn't stay in the position that optimizes the pedaling force. Second, the sole loses contact when the rider pulls the pedal backwards through the dead spot and when he raises his leg. Using just toeclips and pulling the straps tight, from fear of having the feet locked in place, is not a good solution either. It doesn't work if you pull hard and it hampers normal blood flow. The only advantage one could concede to the total freedom of the cleatless shoe would be that it avoids the risk of tendon problems which often result from a bad foot position on the pedal. It's better, however, to learn how to position the foot correctly.

The pedaling movement is repeated thousands of times and a loss of efficiency, be it ever so small, eventually leads to a waste of energy which shouldn't be ignored. If the foot is too far forward the pedal stroke seems more powerful at first but then loses suppleness. This reduces efficiency in the long run and tires the muscles. If the foot is too far back the leg spins well but lacks strength when starting, climbing, or pushing big gears. Therefore, adjusting the fore-aft foot position is critical. You also have to look at the foot position relative to the pedal's axis of rotation. If it isn't correctly aligned it can cause tendinitis of the knee.

To put it simply, we will say that the efficiency of the pedal stroke depends mainly on the fore-aft foot position and that the risk of injury depends on its alignment on the pedal.

Shoe alignment

Those who remained faithful to the old style cleat that was attached to the shoe by the rider himself at the desired place know that there is a very easy method of determining the proper orientation of the slot. You just ride without cleats, using the right length toeclips which serve as a retainer. This leaves a mark on the sole and you then attach the cleat parallel to the mark.

The popularity of shoes with adjustable cleats already attached to the shoe complicates the problem.

There are two possible solutions:
— either remove the cleats, when feasible, and operate as above;
— or tighten the screws just enough for the cleats to stay in

The Look safety pedal allows you to disengage your foot while riding and reattach it just as fast without having to use your hands. The required foot movement quickly becomes instinctive. In the event of a fall the automatic freeing of the foot lowers the risk of serious injury.

In 1985 Bernard Hinault won the Tour of Italy and the Tour de France using Look pedals which he helped design and which helped him avoid falling on several occasions.

Adjusting the Look retention system and checking the play on the axle.

place while pedaling, yet allowing some play. Ride without pulling too much on the pedals. It's also wise to take a wrench in your pocket. The correct cleat alignment will come by itself and you'll just have to mark it on the sole at the end of the ride. Or you can even tighten the screws if you're already sure of the correct fore-aft position.

If you already own well-adjusted shoes it's very easy to transfer this adjustment to a new pair. Take one old shoe at a time, set it sideways on a table with the sole vertical, and measure the angle produced by the cleat and the table. Transfer this angle, usually close to a right angle, to the new shoe. The angle is not always the same for both shoes, since the human body is never perfectly symmetrical. Each of the shoes must therefore be measured independently.

The fore-aft foot position

The theory which has been widely accepted and proven in practice is a very simple one. The joint of the big toe must be more or less in line with the pedal's axis of rotation. In more scientific terms, the point of reference is the head of the first metatarsal.

The first method consists of marking the joint of the big toe on top of the shoe and placing this point slightly in front of the vertical line originating from the pedal axle.

In practice, a certain do-it-yourself talent is useful to successfully complete this operation:

— once you've found it with your fingers, trace the toe joint on the top of the shoe with a white pencil or some chalk;

— find the line perpendicular to the plane of the pedal going through the pedal axle using a carpenter's square sliding on a small ruler which lies on the pedal cage;

— place the shoe in such a way that the edge of the square is slightly behind the mark previously traced on the shoe.

Another method, derived from statistical analysis, has the advantage of being much simpler but calls for a foot that conforms to the standard human foot.

With traditional pedals the cleat must be placed in such a way that the distance between the point of the sole and the slot corresponds to the data given in the table below, according to shoe size:

shoe size	39	40	41	42	43	44	45
distance in cm	10.6	11	11.4	11.8	12.2	12.6	13

For half sizes you have to average the two closest values.

As with any norm this shouldn't be followed blindly but should be tested before it's definitely accepted. There are two ways to do this:

— the first way is to check the position of the vertical line originating from the pedal axle, in the manner we described above;

— the second way is to pedal and to check for yourself, by refining your perception of the feelings around your foot while pedaling.

The perfectionist will find it interesting to make comparative tests by advancing or setting back the cleats. Don't forget, however, that first impressions are subjective when they depart from long-standing habits.

With Look pedals the easiest way is to draw a line on the sole. This line should be correctly oriented and at the right distance, according to the table below. Then position this line more or less vertically over the pedal axle.

shoe size	39	40	41	42	43	44	45
distance in cm	7.9	8.3	8.7	9.1	9.5	9.9	10.3

riding skills

The bicycle is sometimes viewed as an instrument of torture, and it truly is for the rider who struggles in a mountain stage, who gives all he has in a time trial, or who attempts to break the hour record.

This is because of the intensity of effort and the constraints of position which characterize cycling. Great champions can't escape this and neither can insufficiently trained tourists who overextend themselves on a long ride.

Apart from these agonizing moments, the bicycle—even the racing bicycle—is a much kinder machine, as long as you tame it patiently and devote enough hours to the learning process. Your body must adapt to the physical demands. Little by little you'll get the right "feel" that makes the start of every training ride a renewed delight. It then becomes a real pleasure to get on the bicycle, when your first pedal strokes tell you that each muscle is ready to work for the harmony and balance of the whole.

sitting on the bike

Unlike apes, human beings walk upright. But on a bicycle man must learn a different posture and discover that it's no longer the feet but the saddle and the handlebars that support him. The urban cyclist on his old-fashioned bicycle keeps his chest upright. This position has the double disadvantage of letting the whole weight of the body rest on the rear wheel and of offering a lot of wind resistance, which is incompatible with speed.

The real cyclist spreads the weight of his body over both wheels, although a greater load is put on the rear. Even though they seem immobile, the trunk and arms make a dynamic arch in which the muscles regulate tension according to changing situations. At a slow speed or in the pack the arms are almost straight and the trunk is lifted. As soon as the emphasis is on speed, as in a solo breakaway or a time trial, the hands go to the drops, the head sinks, and the chest lowers. This has the effect of moving the center of gravity toward the front wheel and somewhat lessens the pressure on the rear wheel.

This change in position must be accomplished naturally without needing to change the position of the pelvis on the saddle. The pelvis must remain stable while pedaling, and the abdominal, dorsal, and lumbar muscles must be responsive and developed enough to keep the spine straight.

When you tilt forward like this you must try to stretch your back as much as possible and avoid an undesirable hump in the upper part, near the shoulder blades. Such a hump, often found in a rider whose frame is too small, reduces aerodynamics. It also hinders breathing, causes shoulder cramps, and over a long period leads to a deformation of the spine. The cause of this bad posture may be a frame or a stem that's too small. The bars are then too close to the saddle to allow a good extension of the back.

Another mistake, common in Sunday riders but rare in racers, is to put weight on the handlebars with straightened arms. You can keep your arms straight if your hands barely rest on the bars and all your weight is on the saddle. But if you really put weight on the bars you must bend your arms slightly without locking them into position. That way they can act as natural shock absorbers.

Thus, even if they seem to be static, the muscles that ensure the equilibrium of the trunk are always in use. This will keep them fit and even strengthen them in the long run. Also, slight variations of position in the chain of pelvis-trunk-shoulders-arms keep the body supple and responsive.

The optimal position

*T*he only real way to know if you are positioned well on the bike is to be tested in a wind tunnel with heart monitoring by electrodes placed on the chest. I did that in 1979 under the direction of Maurice Ménard near Versailles at the Institut Aerotechnique of Saint-Cyr-l'École, which is one of the most important research centers in Europe.

The extended arms and flat back balance each other like two sides of a roof.

The hands come down to the drops, the arms are bent, the back is lowered.

At speed the upper body is put under tension like the arch of a vault.

Jacques Anquetil had an amazing pedal stroke, pointing his foot down even at the end of the zone of power.

Eddy Merckx, however, crushed the pedals with his heels when climbing as well as in breakaways on the flat.

These tests were preceded by Armel André's studies at Renault's laboratory of physiology and biomechanics. As it turned out, my most ergonomic posture was also the most aerodynamic. When you achieve your ideal position your heart beats slower at a given riding speed, and you feel good because your heart works under optimal conditions. Breathing is unrestricted and it's easier to relax.

The change from my previous position was too much for me to make all at once. Up until then, if I can believe the photos, I sat on my bike like a toad.

It took me six months to get used to my new position on a new frame that was specifically designed for me. Sitting higher and farther back on the saddle, I pedaled more smoothly, especially in the mountains where I switched to smaller gears. The benefits were demonstrated that same year when I won the Criterium of the Dauphiné Libéré by more than 12 minutes.

B.H.

pedaling

Contrary to common belief and despite the apparent simplicity of the movements involved, pedaling must be learned.

This doesn't mean you should force yourself into this or that style, trying to imitate some champion's technique. Everyone has to express himself physically in his own way, with his own personality. You can't copy from anybody else.

But your personal style can gain a lot if you go beyond the stage of instinct, by thinking about the movement itself and doing specific workouts to improve your natural efficiency.

Jacques Anquetil probably provided the best example of this. His pedal stroke was unlike anyone else's, and it aroused the admiration of spectators and of his peers. Vittorio Adorni once confided that he would sometimes get on Anquetil's wheel just for the pleasure of watching him pedal. You have to realize that Anquetil perfected his style in training, with a concentration that often made him resent the presence of other riders around him.

This partly explains his extraordinary domination in time trials. His style was certainly inborn. But he cleaned it up and perfected it, searching for his own best way to put the greatest possible tangential force on the crank during the full rotation of the crank

1

2

The pedaling sequence: 1. Going through the upper dead spot. By extending the knee you can push the pedal forward. The thigh-trunk angle is acute. If the saddle is too low this angle will get too small, keeping the trunk from being flattened when needed for speed. It will also force the back to be rounded, a bad position from all points of view.

In positions 2, 3, and 4 is the power zone. The leg descends forcefully, helped by its weight, and it's easy to exert a perpendicular force on the crank up to phase 3. As soon as this point is passed you must get ready to pull the pedal backward, and it must be decisively pulled back at stage 4 for best results. In 4 the force is directed toward the bottom and the back.

5

6

3

4

From 5 to 6 is the lower dead spot. Thigh movement is minimal. Only knee flexing allows the pedal to be pulled backward. This takes practice because it isn't a natural movement.

From 7 to 8, ideally, the leg comes up while pulling the pedal up. Just being able to keep the weight of the leg off the rising pedal is a definite improvement compared to rudimentary pedaling techniques.

7

8

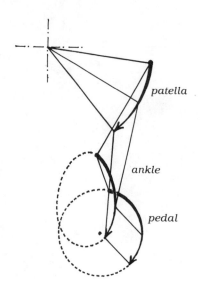

patella

ankle

pedal

1. Power zone

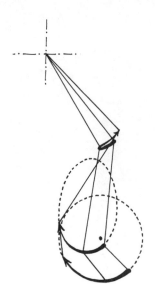

2. Lower dead spot

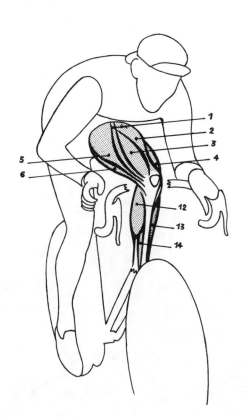

The principal muscles used in pedaling

1. *sartorius*
2. *rectus femoris*
3. *vastus medialis* } *quadriceps*
4. *vastus lateralis*
5. *semimembranosus*
6. *semitendinosus* } *hamstring*
7. *biceps femoris*
8. *gracilis*
9. *tensor facia lata*
10. *gluteus maximus*
11. *popliteus*
12. *gastrocnemius and soleus* } *triceps sur*
13. *tibialis anterior*
14. *peroneus*

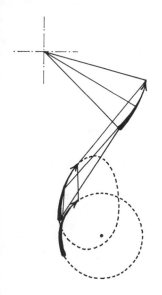

3. Lifting the leg

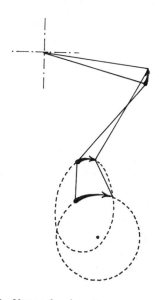

4. Upper dead spot

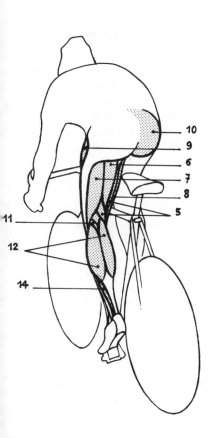

10
9
6
7
8
5
11
12
14

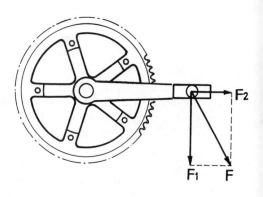

F2
F1
F

The force applied to the pedal can be broken down into two basic forces:
— F1, perpendicular to the crank, that forces the crank to rotate;
— F2, in the crank axis, which wastes muscle energy and doesn't contribute to any movement.

arm. His method also forced him to always have his toestraps tightened firmly.

Is it better to pedal with your foot pointed like Jacques Anquetil or with your heel like Eddy Merckx?

So stated, this is not a good question because it doesn't really take individual peculiarities into account. At best, we can say that it's rare that a rider lifts his heel as high as Jacques Anquetil or lowers it as much as Eddy Merckx. Despite having to spin faster, the Belgian champion could ride more than 50 kph on the Grenoble six-day track fanning a 52x16 with the same foot movement he used in time trial stages in a 53x12. Most riders are somewhere between the two extremes of Anquetil and Merckx.

To pedal well it helps to realize that the ideal would be to continuously change the direction of the force applied to the pedal so that the force would always be perpendicular to the crank arm as it rotates. This is the artistry of cycling and it requires a long apprenticeship. The many muscles of the lower limbs must acquire two contradictory skills—that of exerting the most force possible at maximum effort and of continuously changing its direction. The rider who achieves this just tickles the pedals instead of stamping on them and losing a certain amount of power with each stroke—power whose only effect would be to elongate the cranks if they were elastic.

Given this principle of pedaling it remains for each rider to develop a method that suits him. This comes with appropriate training, during which inadequate solutions will be discarded.

Good riding position is often dependent on good pedaling. Some bad positions can be attributed simply to unpolished pedaling technique.

To acquire good technique it's useful to mentally concentrate on the feeling that the body is carried by the saddle and that the legs are only used as instruments of propulsion. In this sense the rider has to forget about the motions of walking and create new neuromotor reflexes that will give the needed impulse to his muscles. For a rider who likes to use mental techniques—something that yoga and other similar disciplines have introduced to the western world—here is an opportunity to think of himself as a "pedaling man." The rewards are the satisfaction of acquiring a complex stroke and of noticing a definite improvement in performance.

Having established these few general principles we will now examine the specifics of the various types of effort required from the cyclist in different situations.

riding on the flat

At high speeds is it more tiring to ride on the flat or to climb? This is an open question because it's not any easier to break the hour record than to leave the pack behind in a mountain stage like Fausto Coppi did. It's not the same kind of effort. On the flat a rider mainly has to overcome wind resistance and, to a lesser degree, friction. When climbing he has to fight against gravity.

If we ignore the question of altitude, which can be a factor in high mountain passes, we can address the main difference in the effort. This is that a rider going faster than 45 kph has a lot of kinetic energy. If he stops working he'll continue rolling for some time, carried along by the speed he has built up. The climber, on the other hand, would stop quite quickly if he started freewheeling on a steep hill. A rider on the flat finds it easier to get through the dead spot in pedaling. It's not as important for him as for the climber to be applying pressure to the pedals at every instant. The muscles don't work the same way in the two cases. Because of this, it's easier to learn how to pedal well on the flat rather than when climbing.

There are two ways of riding on the flat: spinning in a moderate gear, or pushing a big gear. To ride 45 kph you have to spin at 106 rpm with a 51x15 (7.07 m), the gear Fausto Coppi used in the 1946 Grand Prix of Nations. But only 81 rpm is needed with a 53x12 (9.19 m), which modern riders often use. Contrary to popular belief, it was not Jacques Anquetil but Louison Bobet who started the movement toward bigger gears when he dared to enter the 1952 Grand Prix of Nations with a 52x14.

A good rider should be proficient in both methods of riding on the flat, especially if he wants to do well in time trials.

Spinning

Hallowed by tradition, this method is still worthwhile—it's the foundation of cycling. It's best to learn it when you're young. Then you have the leg speed forever.

The goal is to acquire the muscle coordination that lets you spin smoothly without applying too much pressure in the zone of power while pulling up the other leg. The fast cadence of the spin allows you to save muscle strength, on the principle that a moderate force moving rapidly produces the same work as a bigger force moving more slowly. Because of the speed, your legs and feet have

Above: simulating a counterattack in training, Bernard Hinault goes into a low position to produce his effort.

Below: as he returns to a slower pace he stands up to stretch before resuming the position of a rider in the pack.

kinetic energy which maintains their motion. Finally, the speed forces you to pedal correctly. If you didn't you would pedal in squares and not be able to keep up the fast cadence. This is what they used to call the "soft-shoe stroke," which comes from riding for hours in a small fixed gear. The fixed gear has the benefit of preventing even the slightest pause in pedaling. It helps you to get past the dead spot and to raise your leg.

For this reason Jacques Anquetil didn't hesitate to go down steep hills in a 42x19. This is also a severe test of riding position, because you have the tendency to bounce if your saddle is too high when you pedal very fast. It's equally a test of relaxing opposing muscles while pedaling. Jacques Anquetil also insisted on the importance of thinking of pedaling as a circular motion. You're always looking for the right "feel," as Paul Köchli, the coach of the La Vie Claire team, recommends. The ankle should be very supple, but the speed of movement doesn't allow you to change your foot angle a lot, even though certain riders, like Eddy Merckx, were able to do it. The "ankleplay," dear to Dr. Ruffier in the '30s, comes from raising the knee when the leg comes back up and this carries the heel along.

The advantage of this method is that it's very natural and it develops coordination of the many muscles which work in sequence during pedaling.

Pushing big gears

The use of big gears began in the '50s. Before this the 52x15 (7.21 m) was considered a reasonable limit, even by the best riders. They believed it was impossible to spin with a bigger gear, that it would put too much strain on the muscles and destroy smoothness. In an article in *Le Cycle* on this topic, Jacques Augendre tells the story of the increase in gearing this way:

"In 1943 strong Marcel Kint wins Paris-Roubaix with a top gear of 49x16. In 1948 Louis Caput starts the same race with a 49x15. He breaks away in the early kilometers with a few riders, including Magni and Chapatte, by taking advantage of the southwest wind. Caught near the finish, he says when he gets off his bike that a 50-tooth chainring would have enabled him to hold off the pack. One man will remember this lesson: André Mahé who takes Paris-Tours in 1950. What makes the difference in the last kilometers is his gear of 52x14, revolutionary for those days.

"The Bobet brothers have the audacity to use a similar gear ratio in the Grand Prix of Nations in 1952. Louison finishes first and Jean fourth. Time trials, especially the Grand Prix of Nations, are revealing of the progress made in gear selection because they require high performance equipment. Before Bobet you see top gears of 25x8 for Le Calvez in 1933 and Berton in 1948, of 49x16 for Antonin Magne (1934), of 49x15 for Cogan (1937) and 51x15 (double chainring 51-48, four-speed freewheel from 15 to 18) for Fausto Coppi in 1946.

"After him it's a dizzying climb. Anquetil arrives. He triumphs with a 54x14 in 1957 and a 52x13 in 1961. Raymond Poulidor, who had a smooth pedal stroke, powers a 53x13 (53-49 and 13 to 17) in 1963. This is probably why he leaves Ferdinand Bracke, the future hour record holder, more than three minutes behind. In 1976 Freddy Maertens is the first to cross the 9-meter barrier with a 55x13. Finally in 1979 in his third successful attempt Bernard Hinault experiments with a Gitane Profil bicycle set up with a 53x12 (53-46 and 12 to 17)."

Adapting to big gears provides an excellent opportunity to work on your pedal style.

If you want to go fast in a 53x12, which rolls out to 9.19 meters, it's not possible to use the economical style appropriate for moderate gears, doing most of the work at the power points and following the pedal for the rest of the revolution. That would put too much demand on the hip extensors and knee flexors. On the contrary, you must work at powering the pedal through the complete cycle, attempting to make the effort as continuous as possible by using your toeclips as Jacques Anquetil did.

Since your legs are rotating slower it's easier to change the direction of force, trying to keep it perpendicular to the crank arm. The most efficient way to achieve this seems to be to lower your heel after passing the power point. Roll through the lower dead spot by pulling your foot back. Then lift your heel to bring up the pedal. Finally, tip your foot back at the upper dead spot while pushing forward. This gives a new impetus to the cranks to begin the next cycle. The relatively strong resistance of big gears at medium speed makes it easier to learn this technique. It also strengthens muscles which are not used much by smaller gears. In the end this results in a more supple series of movements.

Using your arms

The skill of riding on the flat cannot be separated from the search for an aerodynamic position, since air resistance is the main obstacle to speed.

Roger de Vlaeminck in Paris-Roubaix in 1977, in a low position with his hands on the brake hoods.

The ideal position would be to keep the chest horizontal, as close to the frame and as flat as possible, with the head down. Just lifting your head and arching your back behind the shoulder blades can make you lose a minute every 25 km in a time trial with an average speed of 46 kph.

To maintain a position like this requires great stability on the saddle. Any forward movement of the pelvis will force you either to lift your chest—and consequently your head—or to arch your back, both of which slow you down. Let's remember here that stability of the pelvis is required for efficient performance. It's the sign of a good pedaling technique, since any unnecessary movement will decrease the output. This doesn't mean you should remain immobile on the saddle. Every now and then it's impossible to avoid an acceleration out of the saddle or a change in position to relax some mucles by changing the amount they work. These changes must be deliberate and not happen every quarter mile.

Your arms are very helpful in stabilizing your pelvis. All you need to do is push on the bars—without stiffening your shoulders, of course. Cycling language only has the expression "pulling on the bars" whereas it should also include "pushing." This image is more correct. Try to pull on the bars while riding on the flat. You'll have to give up almost right away unless you quickly get out of the saddle, which will put you in a better position for pulling. In reality a rider rarely pulls on the bars. At most he'll clutch them when he ascends a false flat, climbs a hill, or scales a pass.

For an aerodynamic position your hands go on the drops at first. But it's possible to bring them up to the brake hoods without changing your chest position and still keep the best aerodynamic profile. Some riders, such as Roger de Vlaeminck, prefer this hand position. It lets your arms and shoulders relax and allows better breathing by opening the chest. In any case, it's a very useful variation which should be alternated with the lower position. The change from one to the other must be accomplished with utmost smoothness, something that can be learned in training. Anything that will scrape off a few tenths of a second in a time trial is good, especially when it doesn't take any extra effort.

Time trialing

*T*o be strong in time trials you have to know everything else first. If you feel comfortable on the bike you'll ride well against the clock. You can work with a competent coach who will correct your defects and give advice on how to go faster. But in the end the most important thing to do is to keep your head low. There are cyclists who always ride in this position, which is also a useful one in break-aways. But I have a tendency to keep my head up to see where I'm going. I take care of the problem of wind drag and turbulences between the head and shoulders by using an aerodynamic helmet.

The role of the arms is very important, but not in the generally accepted sense.

Normally you should be able to pedal with some power without using your arms other than to position your hands and to steer the bike.

In the Grand Prix of Nations in 1984 I was in such a relaxed state that I was practically not even using my arms, even on the Vallauris climb. I was able to wait for the last five kilometers to wrestle with my bike.

To develop my strength in training I do accelerations, once I get up to speed, without holding the handlebars. I take off as in a sprint, with my hands behind my back.

This is a test of good position on the saddle because a poor rider compensates with his arms. To combat his bad position he makes his arms work and loses energy. He would do better to save his energy for his legs.

                                                    B.H.

climbing

As we noted, climbing is different from riding on the flat because the climber must apply continuous pressure to the cranks. Even the slightest freewheeling will affect his speed immediately and noticeably. Gravity pulls relentlessly at the hem of his jersey and his kinetic energy is too slight to compensate for any loss of power.

Uninterrupted pedaling puts a constant demand on the muscles and makes it difficult to eliminate very much lactic acid. It's essential to get out of the saddle occasionally. This allows other muscles to work and lets tired ones work differently. Standing on the pedals also helps in the short accelerations which are so useful in the mountains.

Indeed, our topic here is mountain climbing. Hills can usually be climbed steadily or with a small burst of effort that most road sprinters are capable of. This is true even of long hills, except the endless ones at the end of a race when you have to fight off a fast-closing pack. The situation is different in the mountains.

There are two positions for climbing while in the saddle: seated forward, as many climbers used to, and back, like regular road riders.

Climbing, seated forward

Pure climbers used to adjust their saddles for mountain stages. Before World War II there was even experimentation with a gadget that would let you tip the saddle while you were riding, to make it higher and more forward.

This saddle position is still used occasionally in hilly races for these reasons:

— because of gravity your balance is affected by the position of the saddle in relation to a vertical line through the bottom bracket. On a slope the nose of the saddle is farther back in relation to this vertical line (about 8 mm for a good-sized rider on a 10% grade). By moving the saddle forward 1 cm it's possible to duplicate the conditions of riding on the flat;

— since climbing involves power rather than speed, you can raise the saddle slightly without losing leg speed as you would on the flat;

— wind resistance is less of a factor because you're going slower. So it's not as bad to ride more upright, especially since raising your chest makes it easier to breathe;

— there's less difference between this seated position and riding out of the saddle. This makes it easier to change from one to the other.

In modern racing the flat sections of road between mountain passes are ridden much faster than they used to be, when the tacit neutralization of such sections favored the skills of pure climbers. Therefore it's not advisable to change the bike set-up for mountain stages. This leaves hill races and climbing time trials where this forward position can be considered, the same way as using longer cranks.

Climbing, seated back

The position for flat riding that we described earlier is also good for climbing, especially because the saddle is high. If road riders used to feel they had to raise their saddles for mountain passes, it was because they were often too low by ergonomic standards.

Like Fausto Coppi and Eddy Merckx, the road rider climbs firmly entrenched on the rear of the saddle. He holds the handlebars without clenching them and concentrates on the different phases of his pedaling, forcefully pulling on his toeclips. He climbs powerfully and correctly without moving his hips, taking advantage of the stability offered by his saddle, something that climbers who sit on the nose of the saddle can't always do.

When climbing most riders push the pedals with their heels more than they do on the flat, using more ankle motion. Jacques Anquetil was perhaps the only rider who maintained his toes-down pedaling style on the most difficult climbs, and basically kept his aerodynamic position.

Your chest should be upright, in order to breathe better, and your hands are spread out to each side of the handlebars. Alternatively, you can put your hands on the brake hoods to change the angles of your elbows and wrists. This is a good way to relax them.

Out of the saddle

Riding out of the saddle briefly is helpful to regain speed on the flat or to begin a sprint. But it's on climbs that this position acquires its real value. Abandoning the support of the saddle, the rider becomes a kind of pedestrian and walks with his bicycle, feet chained to the pedals.

Unlike the pedestrian, the rider's weight serves to propel him forward. He puts his weight on the descending pedal, while trying to keep his center of gravity at more or less the same height. This facilitates the rise of the other leg. Up-and-down movements of the center of gravity waste energy.

Climbing out of the saddle shouldn't be an excuse to neglect the different phases of pedaling, especially since this position makes it more difficult to pull the pedal back at the lower dead spot. At best, you can take advantage of the strong impulse that is transmitted to the bike by the descending leg, which provides acceleration. Getting out of the saddle burns more energy than staying on it—this is proven by a slight increase in heart rate—but it also has advantages for the body. Local changes in the muscles' working conditions make it possible to eliminate a little more lactic acid. Even if only minimally, this helps replenish glycogen, which is the indispensable fuel for intense and long efforts.

There are two ways to climb out of the saddle. You can move your upper body from one side of the bike to the other. Or you can move the bike itself, leaning it from side to side and keeping your body stable, so that the descending pedal almost comes under the center of gravity, twice per revolution.

We prefer the second method, which is more economical in terms of muscle energy. A simple alternating arm movement is enough to tilt the bicycle. Your hands hold the brake hoods between the thumb and the two adjacent fingers in a relaxed way. While your hand opposite the descending pedal pushes on the bars, the other pulls on the brake hood. Don't let your body rest on the handlebars, because your weight should be transmitted as directly as possible to the cranks in the zone of power. This series of motions quickly becomes natural once you're aware of it.

The art of climbing

I have often been told that I use gears that are too big in the mountains. I don't think this is true. I always *choose my gears according to the pedaling cadence that suits me. Above this cadence I get out of breath too quickly. Below it, my muscles are too contracted and the blood doesn't flow through them. For me, a good climbing rhythm is somewhere between 70 and 90 revolutions per minute.*

I don't change my riding position except for spreading my arms as wide as possible so I can breathe better. I put my hands at the side of the brake hoods or on the top of the bars as far as possible from the center. I avoid holding on too tightly with my fingers because I strive to avoid all useless tension. Relaxed shoulders, arms, and hands are very important. If you concentrate on this right away at the beginning of your career then it becomes automatic. You have to learn to sense when you're tense.

A rider must discipline himself.

Like everyone else I sometimes get tense on the bicycle, but I notice it quickly. Then I take a deep breath and continue the right way.

Even when climbing out of the saddle I try to be as relaxed as possible. I keep my upper body vertical and let the bike go back and forth. This delivers much more power to the cranks. I adopted this method right from the beginning, rather than moving the upper body to either side of the bike as other riders do. I think I am right.

When you're out of the saddle you should avoid moving your body in all directions, otherwise you lose power. This is also true at the starting line. It's the legs that should work, not the body that goes down only to rise again. I often mentioned this point to my teammates because I like to share what I learned from experience when I'm sure I'm right.

B.H.

sprinting

While it's recommended that you learn flat riding and climbing while training alone, it's much more difficult to do that when it comes to sprinting. Here the goal is to beat an opponent to the line, after an elbow-to-elbow battle that can assume many varied forms in the final kilometer. Without the opponent it's impossible to really sprint. Pure speed is not enough. Like on the track, it's

Above: out of the saddle on a climb.

At right, below: out of the saddle to go hard on the flat.

Below: out of the saddle to relax the muscles.

Pedaling with your chest upright without holding the bars allows you to relax after a hard effort and to rest the muscles which keep the body in a low position. This also helps develop balance on the bike.

not always the fastest rider who wins because strategy plays a major role. Wind resistance is so great at 60 kph that the smallest temporary shelter on a wheel saves energy. This energy is especially precious because it must be delivered at precisely the right moment, down to the tenth of a second. Also, the explosive power of the true sprinter is only available for about 15 seconds, or maybe 20 for those who don't know how to brutally deplete their high-energy reserves. On the road there are even more obstacles:

— the sprint happens after hours of racing, favoring the law of the "freshest" over the law of the strongest;

— local conditions can be infinitely varied, depending on the grade, the width of the road, the surface quality, whether or not there are turns, and the direction of the wind if there is any.

All these elements give an overwhelming importance to tactics, "feel," and experience. Riding technique comes later and is also difficult to explain because it's very instinctual.

What method should you use?

Sprinting technique varies according to the rider, but there is one common element: body weight is used more dynamically. Because of the great force exerted on the pedals, your body rests less heavily on the saddle. This is obvious when you start your sprint out of the saddle and remains true at the moment of the final kick. At this point some riders will sit as far back as possible on the saddle, hands on the drops, arms straight, and literally throw their bikes at the line. Others do the opposite. They cling to the bars, bend their elbows, stiffen their shoulders, sit on the nose of the saddle, and violently push their pedals toward the back.

Gears play an important role.

When André Darrigade deprived Fausto Coppi of a fifth victory in the Tour of Lombardy on the Vigorelli track in Milan in 1956, he beat him at the line in a 50x14, which is barely 7.50 meters. The road rider of that time would sprint with "speed-power," whereas nowdays by pushing a big gear he would use "strength-power," in Paul Köchli's terminology. Freddy Maertens, who was an extraordinarily powerful road sprinter of the '80s, would not hesitate to use a 53x12. That's more than 9 meters.

How can you work on your sprinting technique?

By sprinting.

The learning situations are quite varied. In keeping with tradition the track is always considered a good school. That was where Louison Bobet learned, and he made impressive progress even though he wasn't a born sprinter. The track cultivates pure speed and teaches you how to bump elbows.

On the road there is no reason why you can't improve your top speed by training in a group. In a race, top places at the finish line are hard to come by and will develop your tactical sense.

Technically, we must mention here that you have to be able to sprint with your hands on the brake hoods or on the drops. It's better to have your hands in the lower position because of aerodynamics. But you can be caught by surprise in a sprint with your hands on the brake hoods and not have time to change your position. If the finish line is at the top of a hill, as is frequently the case in mountain stages, it's sometimes better to keep your hands on the brake hoods.

Let us finally remind you that a good sense of balance on the bicycle is a plus for the sprinter, who should know how to "toss" his bike without fear of falling. All exercises which develop the sense of balance are recommended, especially those related to being out of the saddle. These are easy to picture. A good sprinter is an acrobat on the bicycle, and depends on an important safety margin to right himself in case of imbalance. This is why cyclocross is such a good school for sprinting, and particularily so because the rhythm changes all the time. The cyclist who only knows how to ride smoothly in the saddle like a pursuiter won't be able to take part in wild sprints. He's condemned to go from a long way out and ride really fast if he wants to win.

descending

The talent of great descenders is very impressive in mountain stages. A great sense of balance, exceptional reflexes, perfect vision, boldness, and a sense of anticipation are not such common attributes. Nevertheless, it's possible to improve your descending by acquiring a good technique.

The regular road position, far back on the saddle and with a low chest, helps in descending because it's stable and lowers the center of gravity. It's not uncommon to see a rider who ordinarily sits on the tip of the saddle move to the rear to approximate this ideal.

Hands should be on the drops for better steering and in order to be ready to brake efficiently at any moment.

The cranks are usually horizontal so the legs continue to absorb road shock in the area of the bottom bracket. If the saddle and bars are the only contact points your position lacks flexibility.

Keeping the legs together makes them one aerodynamic unit and will help you descend faster.

The feet can feel the forces exerted on the frame and the legs can act as shock absorbers if needed. The pelvis is also better balanced than when one leg is almost extended and the other flexed. This position doesn't exclude pedaling from time to time to relax the muscles, to keep warm, or to regain speed in straight places when the slope is less. You should avoid any stiffness, relax your arms and torso, and not lose the responsiveness without which it's difficult to handle a bicycle well.

Turns are the big difficulty. You should lift the inside pedal so it doesn't touch the road, but keep your legs aligned and parallel to the frame. Some riders extend the inside knee to lessen the centrifugal force. This is a mistake because it increases aerodynamic drag and reduces speed in wide turns where you could go very fast. It's much better to extend your torso slightly to the outside of the turn while shifting weight to the inside arm and slightly flexing the other arm. This puts the vertical of the body's center of gravity closer to the line of travel on the road. It increases the traction of the tires on the road and lessens skidding. This technique is the opposite of that used by motorcyclists. Unlike bicyclists, they can increase traction by accelerating.

Turns that are wide enough can be taken in two ways. The first is to trace a regular curve, utilizing the whole width of the road if it's closed for racing or staying far enough out in the right lane to avoid the shoulder. The other method is to ride a broken line with points of attack joined by almost straight lines. This method is used by Formula 1 racers and lets you descend even faster.

Ready for turning

S ince I started I have greatly improved my style in turns. In old photos my knee sticks out, which is useless and only increases wind resistance. Now I move my chest slightly to the outside of the turn with the help of my arms. Turning comes all by itself. This method is used in cyclocross, where additional pressure is also applied to the rear wheel to achieve maximum traction on slippery surfaces.

I was unaware of this technique when I crashed during the 1977 Dauphiné Libéré while descending the Porte pass. I lost contact with the road and didn't have time to react. Now I use the car racer technique of attack points in turns, whether they're on the flat or downhill. I make an initial change in direction and then go straight instead of follow-ing the curvature of the turn. I repeat this as many times as needed. I don't have to brake and I go very, very fast. I learned this technique at the Castelet. During a race the road is closed. If the turn goes to the right I can then attack it from the extreme left. After the first change in direction I cut the turn close to the inside. When I reach the left side again I turn and continue straight, and so on. It's best to be alone when turning this way, but I've mastered the tech-nique enough to be able to pass other riders on downhill curves.

Above all, a good descender must be relaxed on his bike so he can feel the smallest reactions in a fraction of a sec-ond.

When I want to go even faster on a straight road I hold the bars with one hand and put the other arm back along my body. This decreases drag. But beware of stones on the road! You absolutely must not play kamikaze, especially when there is traffic on the road.

Turning technique on a mountain bike.

Bike handling

P laying on the bike develops balance.
Even a professional will benefit from it. It will help him react instinctively to unexpected situations, avoid crashes more easily, descend and turn better, and sprint with greater confidence.

Our team learns to play soccer on cyclocross bikes. This seems stupid but it's useful to be able to play ball with a bike that isn't made for it.

Other examples?

Doing wheelies, jumping and lifting both wheels at the same time, riding on a wood plank, passing under a barrier, dressing and undressing on the bike, tying and untying shoelaces, and numerous other activities. When I warm up for a cyclocross race I take turns pedaling with one foot attached to the cleats and the other on the handlebars.

On any soccer field there is a railing the bike doesn't fit under. I have fun going under it, riding. All you have to do is lean the bicycle one way and your body the other. I do it on both sides systematically. The human body is symmetrical, and it's important to make both sides equal so you can be agile on the right as well the left. This is very important for the balanced physical development of young people. You should alternate sides even when mounting and dismounting the bike because it's better for muscles and joints. If everything is always done on the same side you'll experience asymmetrical wear and tear as you get older. Balance is innate when you're young and it's made easier by a lower center of gravity. I've seen young racers start completely frozen up on the track, unable even to ride down the banking, whereas little children will go up and down without any fuss.

Daniel Clément is right when he proposes games of balance and agility for children over the age of six and for pre-licensees. They'll benefit from these skills all their lives, including in racing.

Moreover, cycling should only be a game at this age, at least until adolescence. You shouldn't force children to train systematically, whether they're midgets, intermediates or juniors. This doesn't mean you should forbid people to train who feel the need for it. The desire for training must come

Balancing on the rear wheel in the countryside of Brittany.
On his road bike Bernard Hinault jumps and lifts both wheels.

from deep in their hearts. If not, they'll be burned out by the age of 18 or 19 and no longer want to race. Victories should not be important for midgets and intermediates, except for those who train on their own.

As the years go by it's important to maintain good balance and agility, even at the highest levels of the sport.

Roger de Vlaeminck could get into a trolley rail, ride there, and get out of it again without falling. An experienced cyclocross rider, he won Paris-Roubaix three times with hardly a fall. This was not just luck.

B.H.

tactics

by Bernard Hinault

Tactically bicycle racing is very different from running, not only because of the much greater distances involved. On a bicycle you can always recover by drafting someone's wheel. It's important to know how to save strength and use it wisely especially if you're still far from the finish line. So tactics can play a very decisive role.

You could easily be the strongest rider and still lose the race. You learn tactics best during competition.

When I was starting out as an amateur Robert Leroux, who taught me the fundamentals of cycling, used to say to me, "Bernard, you didn't race well," even when I was the first to cross the finish line! And I would answer, "That's not so, I won, so I'm right."

It wasn't until I turned pro that I understood what he meant, because then I wasn't winning races anymore. So I began thinking about all he had told me, and I learned very quickly. On the subject of tactics the advice of Robert Mintkiewicz, my road captain back then, was also invaluable to me.

Basic to everything is having an acute sense of observation. You must be thinking constantly, and that doesn't mean letting your thoughts wander.

There are riders who daydream and who are not really in the race. If someone tells them to attack, they'll attack. If told to do something else, they'll do it. But they don't pay attention to what's happening around them, and that's the most important thing.

There are other riders who might have a good sense of the race, but who don't have the physical abilities to win. These riders often serve as "pilot fish" for others who do have the strength to finish first. And then there are some who learn from experience and others who don't.

As for me, I've learned from my mistakes and I pay attention even when I'm not really in the action. It's become a habit with me. All the top riders in the different teams are like me in that respect. There aren't more than about 20 of them, if I were to pick only the best ones, and I hope the others will pardon me for this somewhat harsh judgment.

training yourself

You have to use your intelligence while training too and strive for efficiency.

The first thing is to set up a program, with your coach if you have one, and to follow it as much as possible. The training sessions should be varied and should follow each other in a well defined order according to your level of fitness and your goals.

When I go out for a ride I have a precise idea about what I'm going to do. One hour before leaving I have breakfast—if it's going to be a morning ride—take care of my personal needs, get dressed, and check over my bike. Digestion is already well underway when I get out on the road.

If I've decided to work out at a high intensity I prefer to ride alone. Every rider has his own rhythm and his own recuperation time between two intense efforts. If you're riding with others you can decide on places to meet, but the training itself is not done in a group.

You can't work out with others when you want to improve your pedaling technique and monitor your feelings. When you're with another rider you invariably want to talk, and you can't work out well. Paul Köchli is very strict about the importance of knowing how to train alone, and I think he's right.

If you're not in particularly good shape it's better to avoid going out with someone who is super-fit, because you would destroy yourself trying to keep up with him.

There's no problem training with others as long as you stay within the minimum or light intensity range. When you have company you don't get bored and you can practice your team-work—taking pace, sitting in—and even simulate a race when you're fit enough. I think cycling should remain a game, one that's fun to share with others whenever possible.

Coming home I never finish flat out. I always save a good 15 minutes for a warm-down on my bike at minimum intensity. It's too bad you can't do this in competition after you've crossed the finish line, at least just for a few minutes. Even race horses are never made to stop in such a brutal way.

learning to watch

During a race, if you want to win, you must observe everything, remember everything, and analyze everything.

In the big tours if the stage is not too dangerous I sometimes have half my mind on the race and the other half somewhere else, but this is rare. Normally when I'm on my bike my brain is working in top gear. Before the race I study the course carefully. I look at changes in direction, the profile, the condition of the pavement, whether the road narrows, and the layout of the finish. During the race I notice the wind direction. It's very useful to have a good sense of direction. With it I can anticipate and change my position so that I don't get caught in a trap in a strategic place. Thus I can easily ride further back but still always be in the good moves. But generally if I want to be in the race I stay between the fifteenth and the thirtieth place in the peloton. Never further in front, never further back.

If I'm in front—and I'm not speaking of breakaways—it simply means that things are not moving very fast. If I'm in back it means I'm not racing, but I'm keeping my eyes open anyway. Everything depends on the stakes and on the size of the peloton.

The course and the weather are not the only things to watch. There are also the other riders.

First I note which are the "easy" ones by watching the way they ride and react. Then I look at those who are really racing or who have a teammate who is a contender. If you see five or six riders from the same team beginning to move forward in the peloton it means they're cooking up something. You have to move up with them to be sure to be in on whatever is going to happen. If you notice a rider who slips into all the breakaways, it means that he's racing to win.

So you have to make a choice. Either you don't move but watch him because you think he's out to block. Or you go with him and help him so that the breakaway takes off.

The intelligent rider who's racing to win makes very little effort until the decisive moment, whether he provokes it himself or whether he simply seizes an opportunity. If you let the stakes get you too excited, you risk working too hard and you'll have nothing left to improve your chances at the finish. I know this, and I've observed it in others, but I still sometimes fall into this trap. Some days I feel the race so intensely and I feel like racing so much that I make mistakes. This can happen in many other areas than cycling. You can be the best and still not win because you've shown your strength too much and have gone out to reel in everyone. In cases like this it's usually a third party who gets the advantage.

None of this can be learned in a day.

You must remember what you have observed. It's rare that I

don't know exactly who has gone with a breakaway. Since I know the riders well I know about how much of a lead I can let them get without jeopardizing my own chances. It's the same thing in time trials and in mountain stages. In the Sarrebourg-Strasbourg time trial stage in the 1985 Tour de France I announced ahead of time how much time there would be between my finish and those coming in right behind me, and my predictions were not off by much.

positioning yourself

In order to keep watch under the best possible conditions you have to know how to position yourself, and to position yourself well you have to know how to watch. The two are closely linked, and I just told you where I ride in the peloton in order to keep an eye on what's happening.

Technically speaking, the goal of "positioning" is to save your strength while striving for the best possible result.

Wind

The secret of a good rider is to find shelter under all circumstances, whether there is wind or not, because it's "relative" wind that counts. When riding fast on a bicycle there's always wind. You can feel it in your ears if you're not well sheltered.

If the wind is coming from one side you must position yourself behind and to the other side of the rider in front of you. Riders in a breakaway who are fighting a wind will fan out, as does a team in a team time trial when there is a side wind.

If the side wind is very strong the fan or echelon will spread out over the whole width of the road, and too bad for the last rider who finds himself in the gutter. If you're riding on the edge of the road the gravel, grass, embankment, and irregularities in the pavement may cause you to puncture or even fall. If a rider refuses to take his pull the others in the breakaway will force him into the ditch to make him change his attitude and do his share of the work. If the entire peloton is confronted with a strong side wind, the first rider to find himself on the edge of the road shouldn't stay there but should work to form a second echelon. If this second echelon doesn't form quickly, and the third, and so on, a gap will inevitably occur when things really get going up front.

A rider moving up in the peloton or in a string should always do this on the opposite side from the wind. It's the same when taking a pull in team time trials.

This is very important in a sprint. When you ride on someone's wheel you have to know how to put yourself on the better side in relation to the wind and come around at the last possible moment, having been sheltered for as long as possible.

Putting the other fellow "into the wind"—without breaking any rules—can work very well. In the peloton a good position is precious when the finish line is just ahead.

Other riders aren't the only windbreak. The course itself can provide many ways of staying out of the wind with houses, clumps of trees, hedges, and fences. You have to have your eyes open all the time, especially in a breakaway, to find protection from the wind.

Hills

Positioning yourself correctly in the peloton before a hill is part of the art of bicycle racing. This is why it's important to know the course in detail, if only to choose your gears ahead of time so you don't make some silly mistake.

Attacks very often happen on hills. If you're stuck in the peloton you don't have time to react. When the line of riders strings out, which happens when the road is not very wide, it takes a lot of time to pass everyone. You can't always know who has gotten away.

So I recommend approaching climbs near the front of the pack. If you're not a strong climber this will help you avoid being dropped as you progressively slip back—but not too much—during the climb then return to a better position on the flat.

Narrow and difficult stretches

A typical example occurs in races which cross northern France and have cobbled sections. If you're racing to win you have to position yourself at the front in the difficult stretches. Otherwise there will be obstacles—such as flats, spills, and other riders slow-

In training, jumping hard out of the saddle with the chest low strengthens both the legs and the lumbar muscles and improves your kick.

ing down—so that it quickly becomes impossible to move up fast enough to make contact with the leaders.

Narrow winding stretches and the tapering of the road often cause the pack to break up—as do railroad crossings—and can compromise your chances for a win if you're in the back of the pack.

These few examples show how important it is to have every last detail of the course in mind, as well as its changes in direction, and to stay aware of the effect of the wind. Memory, observation, and a good sense of direction are indispensable to the cyclist who is out to win. These are all abilities you must work on, even during training.

attacking

If you notice that a dangerous opponent is looking tired, and if the terrain is favorable, it might be worthwhile to attack. Long straight stretches where you are a constant target are not favorable. When you attack, unless you're with some very strong riders, you have to be sure that several kilometers down the road the wind isn't going to be against you because of a turn in the course. I never attack the same way on the flat as I do in the mountains. On the flat you must make a straightforward attack, coming out of the peloton quickly to open a gap. If no one behind me makes a move, and if I'm feeling good, I sometimes just continue. This is the solo breakaway, a sort of poker game in which a knowledge of the time gained helps tremendously in gauging your effort. If there are long steep climbs where the chasers can't make up any ground even if they're pacing each other it's easier to carry it all the way to the end.

Another way is to slow down immediately after escaping from the pack and wait for whoever is going to come after you. At this point I either go on because I want to take them with me or I stop because they aren't the ones I want to have with me, considering their abilities and possible team tactics.

So you have to be able to attack several times. Some days you have to attack again and again before you're successful, by choosing the best spot. It might be the last part of a hill, for example, or a stretch that's exposed to the wind followed immediately by a stretch where the wind is more favorable. In both these examples the gap will open faster because the rider who has gotten away is

Ahead of the peloton in the 1979 Tour de France, Bernard Hinault waits for reinforcements . . . unless he decides to continue alone.

riding much faster while the chasers are still being slowed by the difficult section they haven't left yet.

I rarely have a plan all worked out ahead of time. I decide according to the circumstances. For example, in the 1979 Tour of Lombardy which I won I became aggravated very quickly by the help one of my major opponents was getting from his teammates. I was really feeling good so I said to myself, "Well, if that's the way it is, you're not going to have those teammates around for long. I'm just going to attack flat out and they'll never be able to keep up." That day Francesco Moser was not at his best. When I attacked he was on my wheel and he blew up. Five other riders joined me, one of whom was Bernard Becaas, my teammate. He knew very well he wouldn't be able to pass the other four before the finish. So he worked as hard as he could on the flats and when we got to the bottom of the first climb he said, "Ciao, see you tonight!" So my role was to get rid of all the others. Soon we were only four. I finished with Sylvio Contini on my wheel, having dropped the other three with the continuous grueling pace. I had taken off on a sudden impulse, but after that I managed things very deliberately.

There are no tactics you can apply systematically. It's always unpredictable.

I try to make good use of all opportunities. If my main opponent is in a poor position I attack so he's forced to make an effort. If he doesn't react, he has lost the race.

If I'm in a breakaway where I'm not the strongest, then I do less work and save as much as I can for the finish. When you're not the best it's even more important to ride with your head.

One year at the very beginning of the season on the south coast I won a race ahead of some Dutch riders who were in much better shape than I, because in all the subsequent races I was dropped. I played poker. "I refuse to move a muscle, the others are going to have to do all the work." And when they did, I got them in the sprint. Some days you have to know how to lose in order to win.

This is a game you can practice with your whole team, when you make others do all the work. And when they've done it, they are beaten, if all goes as it should.

counterattacking

This is a variation on the attack which often pays off. After a breakaway, when the chase has been organized and the peloton

On the Domancy climb Bernard Hinault tires out his opponents. Above, he's climbing in the saddle while all those who are still with him are forced to stand up. Below, only a few of them can still keep up. Soon he'll be the world champion.

stretches out, you must stay near the front without working too hard and then jump hard to close the gap.

By this time the chasers are tired just like the riders in the breakaway and the effects of surprise can work before a new chase can get underway.

Like in attacking, you must be sure to choose a favorable spot.

using your opponent

If the course is right—if it has a lot of long and difficult climbs, for example—you can make use of the "law of the strongest" by not attacking all out or at least by waiting as late as possible.

The best example of this tactic is when I won the world championships in Sallanches in 1980. The course included a climb up a long steep hill, one we had to climb about 20 times. Right from the beginning the French team put on the pressure and the race was moving at a very fast pace. On the Domancy climb where I was always at the head of the pack I kept up the pressure constantly to tire out my opponents. My teammates did all the work on the flats.

For the last 10 laps we lost another rider every lap. Finally I was alone with Baronchelli, who was constantly on my wheel. On the climb I rode very hard, but I didn't try to drop him because I knew only too well that I wasn't totally invulnerable. Besides that, there were three Italians behind us, so I had to keep him with me. If I dropped him they might catch us. The best tactic, then, would be to keep him with me until the last possible moment. I had been pushing very hard and he was beginning to get tired. When I attacked on the last climb there was no way he could respond. He simply couldn't keep up.

Often in the mountains I don't really attack. I just pick up the pace until I've reached the very edge of my critical intensity threshold. The riders who are with me try to hang on, thinking I'm going to collapse. But when they crack they lose time very quickly because they have no reserves left, nothing. But if you challenge an opponent openly, even if you drop him for a while, if he has any reserves left at all he can stay behind you without tiring himself out too much. He keeps going and could easily catch you again on another climb or on the flat.

bluffing

You have to hide pain if you're suffering, especially if the race is being decided at that moment. That's what I did in a mountain stage in the first Tour of Italy that I won, in 1980. In the valley we had passed by the Samson ice cream factory and everyone in the peloton had some ice cream, including me.

When we got to the bottom of the pass where I had planned to attack I felt sick. The ice cream was just sitting there. I kept on in great pain and when a rider took off from the front I let him go, unable to follow. Two other riders caught me, and the three of us rode together. I said to them, "Don't worry, we'll go after him later." So I kept them with me. At the bottom of the second climb one of them attacked quite openly and it really hurt me to go with him, for I still had the twinge in my side. That stopped them, though, and they didn't make another move. I was able to hang in until the last 300 meters before the finish and there I suddenly fell apart, I had had it, I lost 200 meters all at once. I sat down on the ground. It was all over, but I had kept the damages to a minimum. If I had yielded ground earlier I would have lost many minutes and maybe the entire Tour of Italy.

forcing the pace

This is the opposite of bluffing. Obviously I'm hurting, but I remind myself that the others are hurting even more, and I win if I am to win.

Sometimes I force the pace at a moment when my opponents don't expect it because they think I'm more in need of recuperation or a chance to save energy for the rest of the stage. This happened in the Tour de France in 1979, for example, after the Amiens-Roubaix stage, where I lost the yellow jersey. I had found myself virtually alone on the cobbled section after a flat, behind five strong riders who were pacing each other ahead of me. In the following days we were at each other's throats. The day before the Évian-Avoriaz 54.2km time trial my whole team and I gave them an unbearable day. There were five intermediate sprints for time bonuses and I fought for each one of them. All the sprints began four kilometers from the finish. It was sheer hell for the others.

The next day I won the time trial stage, taking nearly four minutes from Joop Zoetemelk and winning back my yellow jersey. I must confess I was in really super shape that year.

sprinting

The true sprinter is the one who comes around in the last 20 meters, but with road riders a long sprint is also frequently used.

I'm more of a long sprinter, even though I've beaten true sprinters by using a smaller gear. The gear ratio is very important and there is no margin for error. I've managed to win a sprint because my opponent used a gear that was too large or too small. It all depends on the grade, the pavement, the line of the road, whether or not there are curves—and, of course, on the wind. It used to be that sprinters didn't use big gears, but today it's different. You don't use a gear that you can't push, but it's very difficult to catch a rider in long sprints who pedals fast in a big gear. Even Francis Castaing, who didn't like to use a 12-tooth cog, had to get used to it. Sprinters only put it in the big gear in the last kilometer.

The team works for its sprinter by picking up the pace well before the finish. But there are sprinters like Sean Kelly who have no need for anyone to lead them out, or hardly.

Wind plays a big role. In a side wind you should always jump an opponent whose wheel you were on by coming around on the side away from the wind.

If there's a headwind it's impossible to launch a sprint from way off. A rider sitting on your wheel would have a very good chance to pass you several meters from the line.

If the wind is from behind it's different, because then it's very difficult to come around a rider who is the first to jump hard, as long as he judged the distance accurately. In 1981 I won Paris-Roubaix using the tactic which had helped me get fourth place the year before. I had noticed that the wind was directly from behind. So I had to start the sprint. In 1980 I had beaten Demeyer this way. I remembered this, and I had my reference points on the track. When Demeyer tried to attack from behind, I didn't let

With the help of a tailwind which he cleverly uses to his advantage, Bernard Hinault wins the sprint in the 1981 Paris Roubaix.

him pass, and I won the sprint squarely from the front. Even Roger de Vlaeminck wasn't able to pass me in the last 200 meters. He would have needed a much longer distance to get me.

If there is one area where experience really counts, it's in the sprint. The best school is the mistakes you make as you begin your career. It's better to commit them when you're young. You should try your luck even if you're not particulary gifted, in order to learn.

Bernard Hinault in a time trial—the rage to win.

time trialing

In a stage race almost all the riders who are well placed on general classification will carefully study the time trial course, to engrave its smallest details in their minds.

In the morning I ride the entire course. I notice the condition of the pavement, the turns, the dangerous pedestrian crossings, gravel, drains, absolutely everything. It's as if I were a video camera. Everything is registered in my mind, and at the start the film starts turning. I can push wherever I feel I can make up time without risking a crash.

After 50 km I drink something wherever the speed I have built up will not allow me to go any faster anyway. Otherwise I drink nearly everything at the start and throw away the bottle. Going over the course also lets me ration my effort. Before a hill, where a hard effort will be needed, I can't say I actually slow down but I try to relax as much as possible to save a little energy and prepare for the climb.

At the tops of hills I throw it into the small cog to accelerate right away.

I think one of my strengths is not to slow down on false flats.

preparation

Anyone who participates seriously in a sport, especially if he does any competing—even if only occasionally—quickly realizes that his lifestyle plays a very important role in his success, as well as in the enjoyment he'll get out of it. The dedicated amateur instinctively prepares for Sunday's race all week long. Putting in his miles is only part of it. For him the true appeal of racing lies in competing for the sheer pleasure of it. He's not overly concerned with compiling an impressive record, perhaps because he lacks the physical gifts or even the spare time from a demanding professional life. Competition sets a rendezvous with his fitness, and the joy of improving from one race to another can become the focus of his life. For top athletes, whether amateur or professional, good preparation becomes a prime concern. Knowledge and methods in both mental and physical preparation have progressed dramatically during the past several years.

It is not an exaggeration to say that top competition today has become a virtual testing ground for human physiology, much as the Formula One races have been for the automobile. This testing ground doesn't always get a good press—rightfully so, when you think of the use of anabolic steroids which has already ravaged weight lifting and has since made inroads into other sports. However, as a result of unrelenting rivalry among countries through their athletes, research into improving performance is progressing very rapidly. Once crude techniques can now benefit from a growing wealth of information in a variety of scientific fields such as psychology, biomechanics, biology, physiology, nutrition, and, of course, medicine. Indeed, such a limited list can hardly hope to accurately portray the explosion of traditional disciplines into many specialties. We are now far removed from the weekend cyclist and the average recreational athlete.

But we believe that it's valuable for everyone to be, if not completely up-to-date on all the ramifications of this research, at least aware of some of the essential results. These findings can be applied to the club rider as much as to the independent. We strongly urge the latter, incidentally, to join a club and give up his solitary status. Directors and presidents of associations, as well as the media, have a major role to play in education. That would be a much more positive thing for them to do, if one may say so, than exposing an occasional rider for doping, if,indeed, it doesn't turn out that the test itself was faulty.

psychology

The bicycle racer, no matter how gifted, is a colossus with feet of clay if his psyche is not doing its part, in training or in the heat of competition.

This rather obvious truth is valid for all human endeavor, yet the public probably has difficulty imagining the mental effort required of a successful athlete. For a cyclist to win it's not enough to simply push down on the pedals a little harder than anyone else.

The essential quality is will power. Will power must be used daily to help the athlete stick to his training schedule. It's vital during a race when the competitor is under physical and mental stress. At some point in their careers the greatest champions have all demonstrated an uncommon capacity to withstand pain. It is will power which allows them to control seemingly hopeless situations where others would have given up. Louison Bobet gave the most beautiful example of this when he won his third Tour de France in 1955. He had an open wound from a sclerosis that would have forced anyone else but him to quit or at least to ride out of the saddle for the last week of the race. Not only did he resist these temptations, but he had the fortitude to hide the seriousness of his problem from his opponents. This demonstrates sheer courage every mile of the way.

When courage, will power, and the ability to withstand pain are present to such a degree in competition, it's because they are fostered every day.

Of course, it has been a while since Antonin Magne developed his will power and enhanced his self-image by moving a heavy stone in his backyard every day. It was the myth of Sisyphus revisited, the only difference being that Magne never stumbled under his burden.

The circumstances of road racing have changed a lot since the days when a rider who had an accident carried his broken wheel on his back.

In the 1952 Tour de France the peloton finds time to stop and cool off.

There are two major areas where the human sciences can be useful to condition the athlete's, and hence the bicycle racer's, psyche:

— in his general conditioning, so that he goes about his daily life with ease, despite the demands of his preparation, training, and racing;

— in the use of specific techniques to learn how to relax and to help master the motions involved in the sport and their optimal use in competition.

General conditioning is much like preparation for anything else in life, with certain variations, of course, for a particular sport. The degree of preparation varies with the degree of commitment the athlete brings with him right from the beginning, when he is first introduced to the sport at school or on the playground, and progresses to apprenticeship in top competition. Along the way, the role of successive teachers is very important, starting with the parents. This gives us the chance to bring up the problem of competition for youngsters, which is often poorly addressed. To put it bluntly, but with all due respect to the federations, it's unfortunate that introducing the very young to bicycle racing is all too often only an excuse for holding little races like those of adults. Until a child reaches adolescence, cycling should be no more than a game. Of course this doesn't mean that a child shouldn't go all out once in a while to beat a friend in a sprint, as long as it remains fun. You have to consider, too, the risks to the young if the cardiovascular system is poorly prepared, and the effect this might have on the very intense effort required at a later stage in his career. You must avoid forcing a child into specific training just so he can bring home the winner's bouquet. Yet this is what sometimes happens when, acting as teachers, parents want at all costs for their son to place well or, after a series of wins, to continue to do well.

Like his heart, a youngster's psyche should not be abused. Any adult who begins a serious training program must be careful to maintain a mental balance. You'll admit, then, that the risks are far greater for a child, for whom school—but not cycling school—should be the main focus of interest.

Techniques of relaxation and mental concentration have been around for a long time. Some, such as yoga, go back to great philosophical and religious traditions. It's only in the last 30 years or so that they have been used to help in training competitive athletes, especially in Switzerland. Their success varies. Much depends on the cultural level of the individual, on his motivation, and on the kind of relationship that has developed between the instructor of these techniques and his pupil. We will mention here sophrology, autogenous training, meditation, and yoga, among others.

These methods are used by an athlete either to minimize pre-race stress or, on the contrary, to concentrate on his goal in a very dynamic way. Or, further, they make him aware of the sensations associated with the movements of his sport, helping him learn and improve on them. It's clear that mental concentration and visualization of proper pedaling can help the rider improve his technique and thus his efficiency. This theory has already been proven for other sports, and there's no reason why it should be different for cycling. Some great riders are already doing this. Jacques Anquetil, for example, feels it's very important for a rider to thoroughly grasp the fact that the foot motion is circular. While training alone for the Grand Prix of Nations he concentrated his mental energies in such a way that at the starting line his thoughts were all within himself.

To conclude this section, we will give Carl Lewis the last word. Before the 100 meters at the 1984 Olympic Games in Los Angeles he stated: "Just knowing that I am in good physical shape, that I have trained very well, that technically I am one of the best, and, finally, knowing that I can win, are plenty in the way of psychological preparation."

nutrition

"One must eat to race, and not race to eat," Molière would have said if he had been a cyclist. And not just any kind of food will do.

The question of diet, and especially a sports diet, has given rise to extensive research and experimentation that is beginning to be applied to bicycle racing. Fausto Coppi was the first to make use of the principles of a careful diet, perhaps because his constitution was so weakened from imprisonment during World War II. This kept him out of the peloton just at the outset of a promising career. He had already won the Tour of Italy at the age of 21 and beaten the hour record, though offhandedly.

The large majority of the Campionissimo's opponents didn't learn this lesson. The only exception, perhaps, was Louison Bobet in the '50s. In his usual meticulous way he used theories of diet to great advantage.

A rider like Rik Van Looy was capable of putting away impressive amounts of meat, eggs, salad, and beer before a race. He ignored even the most elementary rules of diet, but this didn't seem to keep him from crossing the finish line ahead of everyone else.

Louison Bobet, on the other hand, used to weigh out his ration of steak virtually to the gram. The night of the finish of the 1953 Tour de France he went off his diet only enough to eat a teaspoonful of mayonnaise, despite his elation at having nabbed his first win in a race which had been so dear to his heart for such a long time. Louison Bobet was a nervous person, prone to anxiety, and, for him, strictness sometimes turned into obsession.

These two examples are noteworthy, not only as anecdotes, but because they illustrate two truths that are important to keep in mind when approaching the question of nutrition. Human organisms differ vastly from one another. They're unique, and it's important to avoid blindly following general rules. Then, too— and this is the most important point—individual psychological approaches to diet also vary a great deal. You have to consider the inner personality which has been shaped by myriad habits from earliest childhood. Jacques Anquetil, who was capable of occasionally overcoming some impressive dietary "mistakes," would never have been able to keep to Louison Bobet's very strict diet. Neither could Gino Bartali—who drank wine—have put up with Fausto Coppi's. Yet none of their racing records would give us an inkling of these differences in behavior.

Yet diet remains an essential part of athletic preparation, as indeed it is in life itself. People who aren't aware of this are victimized by what is perhaps the most astonishing quality of the human body, namely its power of adaptation.

General principles of nutritional physiology

Constantly subjected to a stream of matter, the individual functions essentially as a transformer of energy. As he goes about his daily affairs or, of more interest to us here, as he goes about preparing for competition, he is constantly transforming chemical energy into mechanical energy.

Whereas an automobile burns the gasoline in its tank directly and steadily, the human organism must first transform food into nutrients. On contact with oxygen in the bloodstream, and by other processes as well, these simpler chemical entities are in turn transformed through a phenomenon known as cellular respiration. Chemists and biologists have known for a long time that man does not function like a locomotive burning fuel in his lungs as Lavoisier believed in the 18th century. To simplify greatly, the organism has the ability to break up complex organic molecules. This produces, on one hand, simpler molecules and, on the other, energy. This energy then serves to break up additional molecules, or to reconstruct others which in turn will be broken up to produce energy, or to make the muscles work. It's a curious sort of merry-go-round, with endless combinations. It allows the organism to store energy as well as to release it quickly. And it all operates according to intangible laws over which the individual has no control. This prevents him from acting on a momentary whim.

Herein lies the art of the top-level athlete. He must nourish his body at the right time and in the right way so his muscles will work at their optimum when they're needed most, while still saving the organism as a whole as much as possible.

This is easier said than done. The athlete, of course, is only instinctively aware of these phenomena, and the resultant surprises are what constitute, as Giraudoux once said, "the glorious unknowns of a sport." Can you imagine Fausto Coppi somewhere along that endless 145km breakaway in the 1946 Tour of Lombardy muttering in his beard: "I've totally digested the drumstick I had this morning, and probably the three figs I had at the bottom of the climb, and I can tell that the resynthesis of my adenosine triphosphate is slowing down. Quick, a banana. Meanwhile I'll just shift to my 21."

Yet the muscles' needs are simple enough. Only one kind of energy is needed to contract the muscle, and this is the energy which is released when adenosine triphosphate, ATP, breaks down into adenosine diphosphate, ADP, and into inorganic phosphate molecules. That's all there is to it. The process is made complex by the variety of ways ATP renews itself in the muscle. This depends on the foods digested by the organism, the fitness level, the kind of effort needed, its intensity, its duration, as well as—and this is where the power of the human psyche comes in—how motivated the athlete is. For if it's true that man functions as a machine, it's a machine with a mind! In the section on training we'll examine in greater detail the different ways that ATP is produced. Here we'll limit ourselves to a study of the major food groups and the roles they play in preparing the organism for athletic activity.

Food has a double function. It ensures the maintenance of our bodies—all our cells are born, live, die, and are replaced by others without changing our identity. It also satisfies energy needs, including those of the working muscle.

The three major food groups—protein, fats, carbohydrates—help meet both maintenance and energy needs but in differing proportions, depending on the kind of physical activity engaged in. Thus sugar is not the only food that feeds the muscle. However, the brain uses only sugar for the energy it needs to function. This partially explains why novice cyclists get hungry sooner than more experienced riders whose reflexes are such that every movement is automatic. Learning to pedal makes the brain work.

It's very important to keep the three food groups in proper balance in daily life, and it's generally accepted today that the athlete is no exception. The most that can be said is that he usually has a hearty appetite and, depending on his performance level, is more sensitive to an imbalance in his food intake than the ordinary person. This sensitivity leads to an awareness which, one could say, is the best guarantee against sickness, because the body is alerted before the damage becomes irreversible.

According to Dr. Creff, athletic performance is best if you stick to approximately the following proportions in the daily diet:
— protein 15%;
— fat 30%;
— carbohydrate 55%.

The sources of these are important. An equal amount of vegetable protein and animal protein is recommended, and slightly more animal fat than vegetable fat. For carbohydrates, refined sugar should account for no more than 10% of the whole.

• protein

Animal protein comes from meat, fish, eggs, cheese and other dairy products. Vegetable protein comes mainly from legumes (beans, peas, lentils) and soy products, as well as from foods that also provide starch—such as bread, whole cereals and pasta—and which are therefore grouped with the carbohydrates.

For a long time it was believed that fats and carbohydrates were the only fuels for the muscles. It has since been established—Liebig already suspected this in 1866—that protein, whose main function is to maintain the body's integrity, also serves as a source of muscle energy. This justifies its presence in a pre-race breakfast, especially animal protein which is the only kind providing all the essential amino acids so vital to cell renewal. Even short efforts can benefit from protein because the bloodstream needs a steady supply of it if the organism is to function optimally. In longer efforts it's even more important, and it's wise to be well provisioned with proteins. The drumstick in the jersey pocket for a race of several hours is thus not so silly.

Note that a diet made up exclusively of vegetable protein exposes the athlete to unnecessary problems in the long run. Contrary to a much-disputed theory, this is true even in endurance sports. Of course, an excess of animal protein is harmful, but we're not suggesting that. Here are the advantages of animal protein, according to Dr. Debuigne:

— the presence of essential amino acids;
— a better rate of assimilation;
— an increase in muscle size;
— an improvement in the coordination and regulatory functions of the nervous system;
— better liver functioning;
— an increase.in psychic strength.

Although it's true that people from wealthier countries in the West generally consume too much meat, it would nevertheless be ill-advised to eliminate meat from the diet entirely, especially for athletes. On the other hand, contrary to a well-rooted idea, there is nothing to prove that an athlete should eat more meat than a sedentary person. Current research even proves the opposite. The need for an excessive amount of meat is often simply psychological and the organism, ever adaptable, accommodates itself. Man can get along quite well on 100 grams of meat a day, though some populations, such as the gauchos of South America, eat 700 grams a day without any apparent ill effects. Let's make it quite clear that this is an example not to be followed in our own nation of overeaters.

• fats

Fats are found in meat, fish, and cheese. But basically they come from fatty substances such as cream, butter, and lard from animal sources, and oils and margarine, mostly from vegetable sources.

The energy producing properties of fats are very important, but are not apparent at all levels of output. If it's true that excess sugar always changes to fat—as gourmands know only too well—it's equally true that the organism is able to get carbohydrates from fats with a fairly good return of energy. Since carbohydrates constitute the main fuel for the muscle, this phenomenon has for a long time obscured another fact. Fats can be used directly as a fuel to contract the muscle without first going through any kind of processing.

In other words, whereas it was once thought that the organism didn't begin consuming fats until all its stores of carbohydrates were depleted, current thought suggests that fats are the first fuel to be consumed. The organism is amply provided with them precisely so that it can save on carbohydrates, stocked in the liver and the muscles. The heart, by the way, is a big consumer of fats as an energy source.

An understanding of these phenomena is very important for fine tuning a training program.

Why eat fats at all if they are provided by carbohydrates? According to one general principle of biology, fats have multiple functions. These functions could not be performed by extra carbohydrates even if the carbohydrates could be transformed into fat when not used to provide energy. Muscle fats play an important part in electrical exchanges. They also regulate the sodium and potassium balance from one end of the cell walls to the other. They thus guarantee the absorption of certain vitamins. Even cholesterol, which is naturally present in some fats, is important to the organism. It maintains the framework of the sexual and adrenocortical hormones. Cholesterol is only harmful in excess and it's not at all advisable to expect the organism to meet its basic needs by synthesizing cholesterol from carbohydrates or proteins.

• carbohydrates

Carbohydrates, or, more simply put, sugars, constitute the prime nutrient of the human organism, cyclist or not. They make up more than half of a well-balanced diet.

There are many kinds of carbohydrates, classed according to how quickly they are available to the organism for energy. First come the simple sugars—glucose, levulose, galactose, mannose—which are assimilated directly without having to be digested. Then come the double sugars—sucrose, lactose, fructose, maltose—which must first be digested and then hydrolized into simple sugar. Finally there is starch, which is digested much more slowly, and cellulose, which is not digestible at all, but which, as a fiber, helps food go through the intestinal tract.

Whole grain cereals, vegetables, and fruits contain cellulose. Starch comes from cereals, bread, pasta, rice, potatoes, and legumes. Fructose is present in fruits and many legumes. And sucrose is found in sugar and all sweetened products, and in honey and chocolate.

Carbohydrates, turned into glycogen by the organism, are used in many ways for muscle contraction, depending on the intensity and duration of the effort. Glycogen, stocked in the muscle, is broken down and built up again according to whether or not oxygen is present. It is glycogen that allows you to make your most intense effort, as though the organism were intentionally saving its glycogen supplies when it burns fats during an easy workout. Moreover, glucose, a product of digestion when the blood is being oxygenated, affects the work of the muscles directly. This is why the absorption of sugar during a prolonged workout also helps maintain a sufficient level of glycogen to finish the race well.

Wine, if it's good, can provide a small percentage of the carbohydrate ration. It provides an optimal environment for the digestion of certain proteins such as meat and cheese. But no more than one glass, and only near the end of a meal.

• minerals

A well-balanced diet should provide all the minerals the human organism needs. But an athlete's working conditions—prolonged hard work, heat—can cause at least temporary deficiencies that need to be compensated for.

The sodium-potassium-chloride trio regulates the water in the body, which determines work output. Hence the importance, especially when perspiring heavily, of lightly salted beverages and dried fruits, such as apricots, figs, prunes, and dates to ensure a steady supply of potassium. In addition, potassium gluconate is present in some electrolyte replacement drinks.

The phosphorus-calcium duo should be kept in balance. Phosphorus plays a part in the combustion of all molecules, not just in kitchen matches. It's present in abundance in any normal diet. Calcium strengthens the skeleton, helps prevent cramps, and ensures a number of functions. It's found mostly in milk and cheese, though it's present also in fruits and green vegetables. But it's difficult to absorb. That's why it's better to avoid a greasy diet and emphasize milk and cheese.

Iron is a constituent of blood and absorbs oxygen. Iron deficiency can be debilitating for an athlete, and should be detected with a blood test.

Magnesium plays an important role and is often chronically deficient, not only in athletes. A deficiency depresses the muscles' ability to respond. It can cause cramps and provoke general weakness. Chocolate, bread, potatoes, and dried fruits provide magnesium.

Sulphur helps eliminate toxins resulting from fatigue, and is found in legumes, dried beans, peas, and lentils.

Iodine is a constituent of the thyroid hormone, which regulates the metabolic activity of the cell as well as neuromuscular functioning. Fish, shellfish, fruit, and green vegetables provide iodine.

• vitamins

Without vitamins an organism wouldn't be able to perform the chemical reactions which are necessary to convert food into nutrients. Small quantities are sufficient, and are amply provided by a well-balanced diet. As with minerals, extra vitamins are needed at times of depletion. But an excess of vitamins is useless, for they have no role in producing energy. There are two kinds of vitamins: water soluble and fat soluble.

Water soluble vitamins
These are the B vitamins and vitamin C.
— *vitamin B1* (meat, liver, whole grain cereals, green vegetables) is important for the absorption of sugar.
— *vitamin B6* (liver, egg yolk) is essential for the body's utilization of protein and it improves heart metabolism.
— *vitamin B12* (liver) helps build muscles.
— *vitamin C* plays a well-known role in helping a person to withstand fatigue, cold, and a heavy workload. There is no contraindication for taking supplementary synthetic vitamin C. But foods—including citrus fruits (oranges, tangerines, grapefruit, lemons), as well as tomatoes, cabbage, watercress, black currants, strawberries, currants, and more exotic fruits such as kiwi—should be enough. Potatoes are also a good source.

Fat soluble vitamins
These are vitamins A,D,E,F, and K.
It is advisable to use only food sources. Pharmaceutical supplements can be dangerous, and should only be used under medical supervision.

What I eat

*T*hough I'm familiar with dietary principles and follow them in a general way, I've never been in favor of a strict regime. One should be able to eat anything and everything, or nearly, but without excess. This way my body gets used to functioning smoothly in other countries and in all the restaurants that my itinerant life takes me to. And then, it's not terribly serious to be off form occasionally—except in a race, of course.

Subconsciously I know myself and so I eat what I please, without keeping track of calories.

In the Tour de France diet is not a problem, for they always give us well-balanced meals. This doesn't keep me from having French fries, ice cream, or a little wine sometimes, just for the pleasure of it.

However, when I'm racing there are some very important details I pay special attention to. For example, after the finish, during the recuperation period, I replace my slow-burning carbohydrates almost immediately so my body will begin storing them again as soon as possible, You have to refuel quickly for your liver and muscles. If the race is over around 4 p.m. I'll eat some cereal around 5. If I wait until 7 I've already lost two hours and the more extensive evening meal comes too quickly after.

During a race I drink small amounts every 15 minutes, and don't wait until I feel thirsty. If you feel thirsty it's already too late—you're dehydrated. Your performance suffers if your fluid loss is too great, so dehydration should be avoided at all costs. When I first started racing a bottle would last me about 150 kilometers. But now, for a 300km race in moderate weather, I need 10 to 12 bottles including nutritional drinks. Normally, a rider should lose hardly any weight during a stage, and that means drinking a lot.

On the La Vie Claire team we have all kinds of tea—with mint, lemon, honey—not to mention pure water which will often quench thirst far better.

For breakfast I have been eating less and less meat and more cereals. On the road I eat mostly rice cakes and dried fruits which provide vitamins and minerals.

I keep regular track of my minerals with several blood tests during the year, starting at the beginning of the season. Because I'm high strung I know I lose a lot of magnesium, so I take vitamin D under medical supervision to keep up my level. It's important to be very careful with vitamin D, because it isn't eliminated as easily as others and any excess remains in the organism. Everyone should know his own reactions. For example, I know I should avoid

vitamin B12, or at least take very little, because it consti-
pates me. At any rate, you shouldn't take all kinds of vi-
tamins at random. That's useless. A well-balanced diet
should be just about all you need.

As for minerals, women especially should watch out for
iron deficiencies, for they lose large amounts of red blood
cells during their menstrual cycle. After every blood test my
doctor, who is also a naturepath, gives me herbal teas,
plant extracts, essential oils, and various other prepara-
tions to get me back into balance.
The more I develop, the more I feel that it's important to
look for natural ways to keep in good physical shape.

B.H.

Diet

By diet we mean the overall make-up of everyday meals—breakfast,
lunch, and the evening meal—supplemented by whatever is eaten
during a race in the racing season.

Three kinds of diet are commonly recognized for any sport:

— training diet, which is valid all year and serves to prepare
the athlete;

— competition diet, which takes into account the extra effort
the athlete will be making in trying to win;

— recuperative diet, which facilitates the organism's recuperation after competition.

● training diet

The essential rule to keep in mind is to balance the different food
groups:

15% protein, or about 500 calories;

30% fat, or 900 calories;

55% carbohydrate, or 2,000 calories;

1.5 to 2 liters of fluids, taken preferably between meals.

The total of 3,400 calories is simply a guideline. Individual differences—body weight, appetite, assimilation ability—have to be
taken into account. Contrary to widespread opinion, it's rarely
necessary to increase consumption with training level. The principal effect of training is to develop muscle efficiency, which decreases energy needs. If you lose weight because of a decrease in
the amount of fat stores, it will eventually stabilize because of

increased muscle mass. This phenomenon is a good indication, incidentally, of the quality of the diet and training.

Breakfast is especially important.

Ideally it should be eaten before 8 a.m. and should include, for example, a cup of tea or coffee with sugar; bread with butter, jam, or honey; sweetened cereal prepared with whole milk; and a piece of ripe fruit. Coffee with milk is difficult to digest and should be avoided, though some people have no problems with it if they're used to it. Meat (ham, roast veal, or chicken) used to be popular. But it's recommended less and less by dieticians, except perhaps for heavy eaters or during periods of intensive training.

Lunch and dinner should be as varied as possible according to individual preferences, so we'll limit this to a few brief observations:

— raw or cooked salads are beneficial at the beginning of a meal, preferably at noon;

— vegetable soup is good in the evening, for it helps replace fluids.

General principles of nutritional hygiene should be followed every day: ample chewing to help digestion, sufficient fluid intake especially between meals, fairly regular mealtimes, and attention to the quality and freshness of foods. All this is simply common sense.

Here is the breakdown of calories in a day's diet, as drawn up by Dr. Creff, based on about a 3,000-calorie intake per day:

partially skimmed milk, 0.4 liters
cheese, 30 grams
meat or fish, 250 grams
egg, 1/2
bread, 250 grams
cereal, 30 grams
potatoes, pasta, or rice, 300 grams
green vegetables, 400 grams
citrus fruit, 150 grams
other fruit, 150 grams
butter, 20 grams
oil, 15 grams
margarine, 20 grams
sugar, 30 grams

Fausto Coppi ate regularly during races.

jams, honey, 50 grams
wine, 0.15 liters

These are averages. The importance of this list is to keep you from forgetting anything, and to assure the greatest possible variety.

The current trend is to further reduce the amount of protein and fats, in favor of complex carbohydrates from cereal, pasta, rice, potatoes, and legumes.

Occasional lapses—such as meats with sauces, delicatessen items, and generous amounts of good wines—shouldn't be much of a problem. They are enjoyable when you're with family and friends. And they help your body learn to adapt to all circumstances.

• competition diet

During the competitive season the cyclist spends hours on his bicycle. He eats more than when he's training, because he eats during the race as well as at meals. This is particularly true in stage races.

It's wrong to think you can make up for inadequate preparation by eating miracle foods a few days before a race. Eating is like training. The foundation only comes with time and at least a minimum of seriousness. No concentrated vitamin or magic potion can substitute for good solid habits.

The day before a race, however, you should eat more complex carbohydrates, minerals, vegetables, and fruits—the latter for their vitamins. To keep a balance you can also increase your protein and fat intake slightly, but don't overdo it!

The day of a race you must bring genuine supplements, with thought to the time it takes for them to be assimilated by the body and to the intense work output, which will be both longer and harder than during training.

For races of approximately 100 km, a fairly common distance for amateur races and for criteriums, it's wise to have slightly more carbohydrates about three hours before the start. According to Dr. Creff these should include:

— two slices of bread or toast, with butter, jam, or honey;

— a bowl of cereal with milk and sweetened with sugar or honey, or a serving of pasta or rice;

— chopped steak, well salted, with an egg yolk, cooked with a minimum of shortening;

— one or two very ripe pieces of fruit;
— a cup of tea or black coffee with a sweetener.

Current thinking, however, would say to eliminate the steak and egg and to increase the amount of complex carbohydrates— that is, cereal, pasta, rice, or perhaps a bit of cooked cheese.

If the race starts in the morning you must get up early and eat this meal instead of breakfast. You'll notice that it doesn't include any vegetables. You probably should stick to the three-hour rule unless you have a really good digestive system and you are feeling very much on top of things.

Should you eat during the race?

Yes, but it depends on the distance.

If it's not more than 120 kilometers—this is an indication of length—taking protein wouldn't do any good. Some dried fruit, cakes, and sugar would be enough. A bottle with equal parts of tea and pure fruit juice, sweetened, would round out this snack. Nowdays, however, there are prepared mixtures on the market, sold in specialty shops, that meet the physiological needs of the bicycle racer. Thanks to scientific research going on in several countries, these liquid foods have improved tremendously over the last few years, providing a supplement of minerals as well.

For races of 200 kilometers or longer, it's absolutely essential to eat during the event, and not just carbohydrates. This happens at the famous feeding stations provided by the organizers during the great professional stage races and classics. Riders grab musette bags at certain spots on the course which are selected with digestion times in mind.

There are many stories of strategic ploys where a candidate for a big win skips a feed and breaks away while the pack is slowing down. Fausto Coppi was a master of this tactic and used it brilliantly in Paris-Roubaix in 1950. He won by flying over the course with his jersey pockets stuffed with the necessary food—cakes, rice cakes, honey sandwiches—all furnshed by one of his devoted teammates. When a champion skips a feed it's like gunpowder going off!

Carbohydrates are not enough in these races. You must also take in protein and fat, as well as a small amount of vitamins and minerals. This maintains your body's reserves at optimal levels and assures good intercellular exchange.

Several choices are possible, depending on individual taste and on what technical support is available for riders to depend on. Like jersey pockets, musettes can carry solid foods which are easy to eat and digest while riding. The menu used to rely heavily on protein and fats—small ham sandwiches, pieces of chicken, or customized meat pâtés made with meat, liver, egg yolk, flour, and sunflower margarine. Today you would add an increased proportion of cereals and sugars provided by such things as gingerbread, rice cakes, toast, crackers, and dried fruits (raisins, figs, apricots, dates, bananas) which work well because they are small. You would also take fresh fruit (bananas, apples, oranges, tangerines) for the liquid content. And don't forget sugar lumps. Over the last several years, complete liquid meals have appeared on the market which can substitute for natural products. They have the advantage of being homogenized— that is, "balanced" from the first to the last drop. And they're easy to absorb and digest, as long as you don't gulp down a whole bottle all at once.

These ready-made complete liquid meals could also serve as a replacement for the pre-race meal, provided the race is around 100 kilometers. Because they are absorbed during the course of the race, these foods don't mean you can do without sweetened beverages—which usually also provide vitamins and some minerals—or water, of course. This is true not only in hot weather. Maintaining a constant and sufficient liquid volume is crucial for physiological efficiency. You have to drink frequently and before you're thirsty—a little bit every quarter of an hour, for example. If there is significant water loss, output can be reduced by as much as 25%.

This brings up the question of how many bottles to carry on the bicycle. For riders who have a support crew there's no problem, especially not if they're also being protected by a teammate.

On the La Vie Claire team, riders always have a choice of three kinds of bottles:

— bottles of tea, sweetened or unsweetened, with different flavors (lemon, mint, plain);

— balanced liquid foods;

— bottles of pure water.

If you're planning a long ride by yourself, you should have two bottle cages on your bicycle, one for liquid food and the other for a beverage.

● recuperation diet

After a long, hard race the exhausted rider is in a state that could, from a certain point of view, be considered a benign illness. When they're sick, animals eat less or even stop eating until they've recovered. However, the tradition in the world of sport is for the athlete to consume an even richer and bigger meal, with plenty of wine. Even if the joy of sharing this little gastronomic feast with friends lessens the drawbacks by noticeably improving digestion and absorption, it is still a dietetic error. The fact is that before recuperation can take place the organism needs to get rid of toxins by eliminating nitrogen residue which has built up during the race.

There are two phases:

— "detoxification," a 24-hour period during which you should rehydrate yourself with water which includes minerals. Right after the race it's advisable to drink a quarter of a liter or more of soda water or bicarbonate of soda with one gram of sodium chloride and a half gram of potassium gluconate. Preferably this should not be iced, and don't drink it all in one gulp. One hour after the finish, you should eat some cereal to reload your system with complex carbohydrates.

Food thereafter should be limited in protein and fat. Sugars and starches will provide the slow-burning carbohydrates.

— "restoration," extending over a 48-hour period, requires about 40% more intake than the training diet but keeps the same proportions, especially for protein.

Three days after the race you should go back to your training diet.

Carbohydrate loading

Specific preparation for certain events, such as time trials like the Grand Prix of Nations, has put the spotlight on a special diet. It's called carbohydrate loading and was developed by Scandinavian researchers several years ago.

The principle of it is simple. The goal is to force the body to store more glycogen than it usually does from its normal diet. You begin by depriving yourself of any carbohydrates for a few days, so that your body builds up a need for them. This need is then satisfied by eating carbohydrates exclusively during the days immediately preceding the event. The human organism reacts just like the prudent housewife who cleans out the supermarket shelves when a product shortage threatens. Indeed, the muscles' glycogen reserves are multiplied up to 15-fold in the most successful cases.

In order to empty your muscles entirely of their glycogen, you must put in a workout of a least two hours the first day without eating any carbohydrates. This should be between a light and a medium workout on Paul Köchli's scale—that is, at about 80% to 90% of VO_2 max, as we will see a little further on.

The second and third day, still without carbohydrates, you go riding again. You won't be able to work very hard because you'll be feeling the lack of fuel.

Then for the next three days carbohydrates become the main part of your diet. By the day of the race you'll have so much glycogen stored in your muscles and liver that you'll be able to work much harder and improve your performance.

Despite much experimentation on the subject, it has not yet been irrefutably proven that performance is improved under this regime. It can be stated, however, that some athletes seem to derive a quite obvious benefit, others do not.

Not all individuals can stand the shock to the system, psychologically or physiologically. Motivation plays a large part, as does support from the circle of family and friends. The rider is constantly prey to passing temptations that can compromise the results.

Carbohydrate loading should be considered with a particular competition in mind and under the supervision of a qualified coach. Many variations are possible, and this is why we will not be more specific about the procedure.

Carbohydrate loading is not recommended for the average amateur, yet it shouldn't be prohibited for those who enjoy experimenting on their own bodies to discover and study its reactions. Time trialing really lends itself best to this very special preparation.

Carbohydrate loading

and the

Grand Prix of Nations

*I*n 1984 I won the Grand Prix of Nations, a 92km time trial in Cannes, after carbohydrate loading. The principle of this is well known. You deplete your system of carbohydrates for a short period while continuing to train, thus starving the muscles. Though there will be a moment where you feel totally "out of gas," you must continue a little longer so that your body is depleted of as much glycogen as possible. After this you begin to eat as many carbohydrates as possible, cutting out protein and fat. Because it was deprived, the body reacts by stocking up even more than usual, for fear that it won't get enough. After that, all you need to do is have one normal meal, and you are all ready for your race.

There are several ways of going about carbohydrate loading. Here's how I went about it in 1984 under Paul Köchli's supervision:

— on Wednesday I raced Paris-Brussels, nearly 300 kilometers. For 200 kilometers I ate what I always do, but during the last 100 I didn't eat at all, though I drank some water. That evening I had no carbohydrates for dinner;

— on Thursday I had a good workout of several hours on the road. I didn't eat any carbohydrates on my ride or at meals, but I drank a lot;

— on Friday I didn't have the tiniest bit of carbohydrates until 4 p.m. I took a 30km ride and could hardly go further. At 4 p.m. I reversed the procedure, eating a maximum amount of carbohydrates, both simple and complex. One hour later I did 30 kilometers at an easy pace;

— on Saturday I rode a bit and ate carbohydrates all day. In the evening I began eating protein and fat again, but in small amounts;

— on Sunday morning at 8 o'clock I had a balanced meal. Before going out to ride the course as a warm-up I had some more carbohydrates. For the noon meal, before the race, I wanted to eat normally but found I was hardly hungry at all. I ate just a little protein and fat before the race. I then proceeded to win the race, beating my previous record.

That was the only time I tried this regime.

I don't recommend this for everybody. It must be done under very special conditions, with good support, because it's hard to keep to. It's only useful if the race will have a definite pace to it, as is the case in a time trial. I've seen riders try carbohydrate loading for a one-day classic. The pace wasn't fast. They finished with their reserves barely tapped, without having been able to do anything. What you are aiming for is to have resources you can draw on when everyone else is burned out. In a mass start race this only works if you can be in control, by breaking away or by using your opponent, but you have to be very strong. On *a course like Sallanches, the site of the 1980 world championships, carbohydrate loading would have worked very well.*

B.H.

training

Cycling is one of the sports where training brings the willing athlete the greatest opportunity for improvement. This is because of the important role played by the acquisition of a very specific skill—that is, pedaling—and because of the great endurance that must be developed, at least for road racing. The term "endurance" is used here for convenience before getting into more precise terminology for the different kinds of effort required in cycling. It's merely meant to point out that major bike races cover 250 km or more, and can last more than 8 hours. Among the problems—but not the only one—confronting the racer is being able to "go the distance."

Distance is the oldest method used to evaluate a cyclist's training. You simply keep track of the number of kilometers covered in each training session and the total amount over a given period. The kilometers ridden give an initial indication of the cyclist's degree of fitness, but this is valid only for a rider who knows how to train and who puts in these distances at the beginning of the season according to a prescribed format. It's generally estimated that it takes 2,000 to 3,000 km for a rider to begin to be competitive again after the winter break from racing, a break which increasingly includes other sports and physical activity. But if these distances were to be covered at a uniform speed of 25 kph the results would be only mediocre. In reality a cyclist doesn't take the same sort of training rides at the beginning of this period of getting back into shape as he does at the end.

Though it's a rather inexact mechanical comparison, you only have to think of the breaking-in period of a car in order to understand it. While you're breaking in the engine it's recommended to increase cruising speed now and then for variety by accelerating on the downhills. That way you're not putting too great a workload on the moving parts while there's still a lot of friction. Later you do the same on the flats. Everyone knows there's nothing worse than forcing an engine that's still "tight" by going uphill in fourth gear without having picked up speed.

The experienced cyclist who knows how his body reacts will get on the road around the middle of January. Little by little he'll increase the speed and distance of his rides. But he'll also accelerate to a higher level for increasingly longer periods, so he can regain his ability to break away repeatedly and to stay away alone.

It should be clear, then, that the number of kilometers alone is not the way to define a training program, but it's useful for keeping track of rides. The traditional little diary in which you carefully record the distances you cover during the week is worth keeping up to date, especially if you also note the kinds of effort used and some impressions of your fitness. This kind of discipline helps the mental conditioning of a rider who takes his basic preparation seriously.

"Going the distance" has no meaning except in competition. Though it's true that a rider accustomed to 80km races will have some trouble in a 120km event, this is due to the repetition of the effort over a longer period of time and not to the increase in mileage. Louison Bobet understood this well and preferred to speak of hours in the saddle rather than of kilometers covered. This is especially the case during the season, when the body is functioning optimally.

It's true that bike tourists who want to prepare for rides of 400 km or more should gradually increase their distances during the preceding weeks. But since they almost always ride at the same speed, their kilometers convert very accurately into hours in the saddle . . . and we are back again to the idea so dear to Louison and Jean Bobet.

Until the past few years there was a prevalent theory that a racing cyclist's conditioning was dependent on two complementary qualities. One was endurance, which was said to allow him to ride a very long time at a good pace. The other was power, which would allow him to make violent efforts repeatedly, as, for instance, when he attempted to drop someone riding on his wheel. All attention focused on the changes occurring in the athlete's heart. It was assumed that power would strengthen the heart wall and that endurance would increase its volume. The art of training consisted of balancing these two phenomena. Particular care was paid to youngsters, for fear that the walls would strengthen too quickly before the heart had reached a sufficient volume. This would block its optimal development.

More recent work in sports physiology has shown that these notions didn't account for what's really going on and could not be used as a basis for programming a racer's training.

As far as we know it was Paul Köchli, coach of the La Vie Claire team, who introduced more precise concepts on this subject, and we'll be referring to these constantly throughout this chapter. As he himself stresses in the advice he heaps on the team members, it's impossible to describe correctly what's happening on the road without a specialized vocabulary. We have decided to use this specifically adapted vocabulary.

Training workload

The principle is the same for all sports. The athlete voluntarily submits his body to a given workload, selected with a particular goal in mind, and persists beyond the initial fatigue which would ordinarily cause someone to quit. He recuperates between two sessions—or else between two successive exercises if it's repeat training—and begins again, with the idea of increasing the workload even if only slightly. "More than yesterday, less than tomorrow." This old saying of lovers everywhere has become the athlete's motto as well. Love of sport is not an idle phrase. The most curious thing is that it all happens as if the body in some way understands the message it's receiving. For during the recuperation phase it prepares itself to bear a heavier workload than before. This has the effect of raising the pain threshold, which acts as a safety valve. The athlete's body seems to be thinking: "You got me that time, but you won't next time around. I'll be ready for you!" But the next training session is even more challenging. And patiently, enthusiastically, or just resignedly the body obeys—within its own physiological limits, of course.

Thus, the principle behind training is to systematically and progressively increase the workload, by lengthening its duration or by increasing its intensity or by increasing the number of repetitions. There are many possible combinations. The maximum intensity of athletic performance is different for each individual, and varies with training. It's convenient to express all intensity of effort as a fraction of maximum intensity, an intensity which can only be sustained for a very short time. Duration and intensity vary in inverse proportion for the different kinds of effort. These can be classified in types, not only according to the efforts made in a road race and in the whole track racing repertory but also to the ways that the body's metabolism functions.

Exercise intensity levels

Paul Köchli identifies six levels of exercise intensity that we shall introduce here, giving as much information as possible on the physiology of each and on the signs that help you recognize them while riding. In setting up an explicit hierarchy of these various intensities we'll be using some words in a very specific way that won't necessarily correspond to their ordinary usage. In this terminology, for instance, the hour record fits under the heading of "light" intensity even though in the last few minutes it quite likely reaches into the "medium" intensity, the area of the 5,000m professional pursuit.

A preliminary remark is needed. Whatever metabolic processes are set to work by the organism (and these depend on the conditions surrounding the racing cyclist at the moment he produces his effort) the muscle uses only one "fuel," adenosine triphosphate, commonly known in scientific works as ATP. This breaks down into adenosine diphosphate (ADP) and other compounds, thus freeing energy for muscle contraction. Another organic compound, phosphocreatine, which is also present in the muscle cells, combines with ADP to make new ATP, which is again broken down by the next contractions. It only takes a few seconds. ATP and phosphocreatine supplies are restored by the organism as much as they can be through processes that take place just as easily at times of less intense efforts—i.e, partial recuperation—as during complete rest. These processes are even more effective if the nutritional intake has been correctly balanced and if training has been well managed.

- **minimum intensity**

Work at minimum intensity can be easily sustained for several hours.

The energy is provided by the burning of lipids—that is, fats—which are transformed as they come in contact with the oxygen transported by the blood. In other words, we are talking here of aerobic metabolism, for oxygen is provided by the air breathed in.

It's interesting to note that the organism doesn't use carbohydrates first even though they're the muscles' favorite food. The organism acts as if it wanted to retain the carbohydrates it already has (in the form of glucose in the blood and as glycogen in the liver and in the muscle cells) for the time when the body will be making a more sustained effort that will require their oxidation.

The transformation of fats—in the form of free fatty acids—requires more oxygen than does the transformation of carbohydrates so it's logical that it happens at a time when the athlete is breathing easily and working less.

The range of minimum intensity is figured at 20 to 40% of maximum intensity, which means a heart rate of between 65 to 80% of maximum. We know that maximum heart rate varies from one individual to another, not only with age. So it's important to know your maximum so you can gauge your work intensity by taking your pulse. We'll return to that.

There's another fairly simple way to find out if you're going beyond the minimum intensity range and into the next range, light intensity. Breathing becomes harder, so you find it more difficult to chat with your friends. You are crossing what Paul Köchli calls the "gossip" threshold, a good image which will undoubtedly call to mind some very concrete memories of discussions that were cut short because of a group ride speeding up.

If you want to lose some extra pounds—for health reasons or to improve your fitness—riding at a moderate pace and breathing deeply will help you lose weight most easily as long as you go out for several hours and don't eat too much. If you want to lose even more weight you must also work out at light intensity so your body will use up carbohydrates which would otherwise turn into lipids—i.e, fat.

• light intensity

When the oxygen intake is not enough to transform fats, it's time for carbohydrates. First to be used is the glucose contained in the blood—if you've been eating correctly before the ride—then the glycogen in the muscles and finally the glycogen in the liver.

So the organism changes its fuel, although the muscle itself continues to function with adenosine triphosphate and phosphocreatine, which are closely linked because of the way they constantly convert into each other.

Light intensity means from 40 to 50% of maximum intensity, which translates to a heart rate of 80 to 90% of maximum. For an athlete who can reach 200 beats per minute, this would mean 160 to 180 bpm, already a high rate.

A cyclist who is well trained and well prepared can remain at light intensity longer than a half hour, and the effort required is significant. His body must not only have good carbohydrate reserves in different forms, but must also be able to burn them without going into oxygen debt which would put him right into an anaerobic state. Light intensity is characterized by a maintaining of aerobic metabolism. But you are already flirting with anaerobic functioning, in which your body would no longer get the energy necessary to resynthesize adenosine triphosphate from oxidation alone.

What feelings tell you that you're going to cross into the medium intensity range, the next category? Muscle discomfort is one and, above all, it will become more difficult to control breathing. As long as you remain in the light intensity range you must breathe deeply—you can't talk at all—in order to absorb the maximum amount of oxygen, oxygen which is used up completely. But you can still follow advice on breathing technique from your coach. Beyond this point, it would become impossible. This is the best possible time to use breathing techniques because of the great need for oxygen. This is the last stage where the well-trained rider can still concentrate on breathing.

• medium intensity

In order to find the energy the muscle needs without using only oxygen—it's already being used—the organism now breaks down glucose and glycogen by another process. This process, called anaerobic glycolysis, is more complex and less efficient and it causes lactic acid to be produced. Lactic acid builds up in both the blood and the muscle cells, giving rise to greater and greater pain which forces you to stop after a while or to decrease the intensity. At that moment lactic acid is converted, at least partially, back into glycogen. This form of recuperation occurs more rapidly if the intensity level falls back to minimum. This happens, for example, when the rider slips back into the peloton and remains there for a while sitting in.

Medium intensity occurs between 50 and 60% of maximum intensity with a pulse of 90 to 100% of maximum. At this heart rate, the effort can be maintained from 4 to 30 minutes in the range we're considering. Anaerobic glycolysis accounts for only about a third of the energy freed. The other two thirds are provided by oxidation. It's in the intense part of this range that the cyclist reaches his maximum oxygen uptake—called VO_2 max—which indicates his ability to perform an all-out effort for the longest possible time. In a well-trained athlete the threshold between light and medium intensity is between 80 and 90% of VO_2 max oxygen consumption. Eddy Merckx passed this threshold at 100%, which partially explains his racing achievements. One of the first goals of a cyclist's training should be to raise his initial threshold, which will lead to a corresponding increase in his VO_2 max itself.

VO_2 max cannot be reached until you have begun to call on the anaerobic process. That's because the resulting lactic acid, together with carbonized gas, is the main stimulus to the cardiovascular and respiratory system, which need them to function at full throttle.

At this intensity, according to Paul Köchli's apt saying, "you don't breathe any longer, you are breathed." This underlines the importance of first acquiring a good respiratory technique.

When a racer is working at medium intensity, he is teaching his body to prolong its effort at VO_2 max and to hold this pace for 11 minutes, for example, instead of only 6.

• high intensity

The aerobic oxidation of carbohydrates and their anaerobic glycolysis play an equal role here in the production of energy for durations not exceeding 2 to 4 minutes. The heart beats at maximum frequency.

High intensity represents 60 to 70% of maximum intensity.

• submaximum intensity

Aerobic oxidation is greatly reduced here, but still contributes a little to performance which is carried out in a much smaller time frame, between 25 seconds and 2 minutes. The flying start kilometer is contested at submaximum intensity, with the heart beating at its maximum. In road races this intensity can be reached during a violent acceleration or a long sprint at the finish. The organism goes into "oxygen debt" because the energy deployed is greater than the amount furnished by the air breathed in. The racer must interrupt his effort—by sitting on an opponent's wheel, for example—so that he can recuperate. There he builds up some reserves of glycogen again by burning part of the lactic acid that has accumulated in his muscles during the violent effort he has just made. A well-planned training program would help a rider reduce the time needed for this partial recuperation. Cycling is the sport which offers the best example of this process because at high speed the effort needed to stay on a wheel is much less than that put out by the rider in front. The tactics you see in a small breakaway group a few kilometers from the finish are entirely dictated by the physiological phenomena we've just described.

Everything we've said about recuperation from submaximal in-

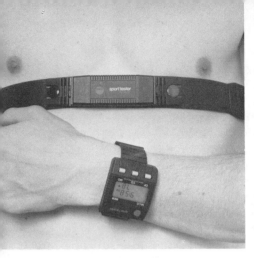

A simple belt around the chest.

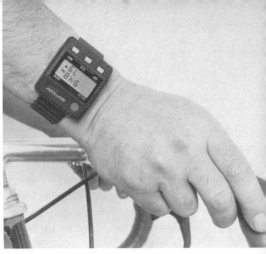

The Sport-Tester heartrate monitor on the wrist.

At the finish the Sport-Tester case processes the information registered by the monitor.

The apparatus draws a graph of the heart rate, a precise image of the work done during training.

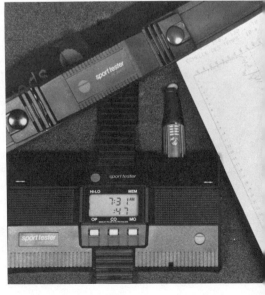

tensity is obviously also valid for high intensity and even for medium intensity, if applied to road racing. As soon as lactic acid rises to a significant level, recuperation time is indispensable for its reconversion. Medium and high intensity are called into play, for example, when a breakaway group wants to widen the gap, or on the edges of the peloton. The rider who gets dropped because he doesn't have sufficient anaerobic capacity is irremediably left behind. The minutes he falls behind add up very quickly, because it's impossible to ride for very long alone at high intensity or even at medium intensity. This observation is valid for team time trials where the riders are repeatedly flirting with high intensity. The weaker ones, or the most fatigued, must skip a pull or drop off even though they could easily stay with the pack if the leaders were riding at light or medium intensity.

• maximum intensity

This is the intensity of the all-out sprint, for a period that can be as long as 25 seconds. The range is from 90 to 100% of the individual's maximum. The heart beats virtually at its maximum, needless to say.

There is a very particular metabolic process here which departs totally from all the preceding ones. The aerobic and the anaerobic glycolysis processes are too slow. The organism needs faster sources. It thus resorts to the muscles' reserves of adenosine triphosphate which it breaks down without using any of the oxygen breathed in. Then it recomposes this in order to redecompose immediately, using its reserves of phosphocreatine.

We talked about this mechanism before discussing the levels of intensity. To be precise, it means total effort for a time during which the athlete doesn't even have time to breathe. Breathing wouldn't do him any good anyway since the chemical reactions at work are anaerobic. There is nothing in common here with anaerobic glycolysis which hurts the muscles. If you stop an all-out sprint within the time mentioned the only effect you'll have is the feeling that you have nothing left. Total effort would be of a higher quality after a light warm-up that opens the capillaries and maximizes the speed at which intercellular exchanges take place. It's true that a sprinter doesn't prepare for a 200-meter flying start by putting in 100 km on the road. But this kind of effort could very well be produced with whatever is left in the muscles at the end of a race like Paris-Roubaix, if the sprint is very short. If it's a long sprint the glycogen reserves will quickly come into play by anaerobic glycolysis. That's what usually happens.

Learning to know yourself

The purpose of a training program is to make the rider work at different intensity levels to develop the qualities he needs in competition.

In the past these programs formally consisted only of the number of kilometers to be covered on certain days of the week, with occasionally a very general suggestion—an easy ride, endurance work, speed work. It was up to the experienced rider to adjust his pace according to what he knew about himself and his goals. Fausto Coppi, for example, ended his training rides with an actual 5km flat-out time trial. He deliberately broke with the interminable 200km rides at 25 kph that were so dear to road racers of his day. Without realizing it they were working at minimum intensity and training only their endurance. Thus they were teaching their bodies to postpone the point at which aerobic oxidation of fats changes to that of carbohydrates. That's useful, but it's not enough for modern competition.

The great champions have an instinctive awareness of their physiological state when working out, and they've refined this through their experiences in competition. They remember the lessons of the mistakes they've made and they know how to adapt their tactics to the strength they have left.

Nowdays it's possible to gain such experience more quickly. All you have to do is work attentively in the intensity ranges that we've defined here, especially at their highest limit, so as to raise the thresholds between them. This will help you save your body's reserves while achieving the same output on the road.

For that you need to know the duration and intensity of the training workloads.

You can get a good idea of the intensity from your heart rate, which you can monitor at any time if you have one of those heart-rate monitors that are on the market these days. Equipment like this, especially for a beginner, is a hundred times more useful than super-light components. These latter are very expensive and much less helpful than understanding when you are passing from one threshold to the next. With a little practice you can always monitor your pulse while riding by feeling the carotid artery for 15 seconds and multiplying by 4. It's not very convenient—especially not when riding on cobblestones—and it can interfere with maintaining a flat-out effort in an aerodynamic position. Coupled with an electronic speedometer, the heartrate monitor proves to be a very valuable tool. With practice, just knowing your speed and what gear you're in is enough for the experienced rider. It's an education you have to go through, and electronics can make it a lot easier.

The way you breathe is another important consideration. The gossip threshold, somewhere between minimum and light intensity, pinpoints your endurance level. It's based on using aerobic metabolism of fats as long as possible, thereby economizing glycogen reserves.

The threshold where all conversation ceases, somewhere between light and medium intensity, pinpoints the level of aerobic metabolism of glycogen. Raising this threshold postpones the switch to anaerobic glycolysis that causes lactic acid.

A rider whose anaerobic threshold is higher than his adversaries' will be in a state of relative recuperation much more often— for example, sitting in—and will finish fresher, giving him a big advantage as he approaches the line.

The threshold where control over breathing is lost, at medium and nearing high intensity, is hard to maintain because of muscular distress and difficult breathing due to oxygen debt. Riding at this threshold allows you to increase your anaerobic capacity, also called power, on which your ability to produce intense and prolonged efforts depends. Without this it would be virtually impossible to maintain the 50-meter lead you need to win a race alone ahead of a peloton that's out to catch you.

Training methods

Duration and intensity of effort, which are interdependent, produce their desired effects on the rider's body during training and should be taken into account when setting up a program.

The problem is complicated by the fact that the same training session has to include different levels of output—unless you always ride at the same speed the way tourists do, at minimum intensity, which won't develop the qualities you need for competition. You must incorporate some ultra-short sessions at high, submaximum, and maximum intensities—2 to 4 minutes, 25 to 120 seconds, 10 to 25 seconds respectively—as well as relatively brief sessions of up to 30 minutes in light and medium intensities. Training methods actually depend on the sequence and duration of periods of more or less complete recuperation, which allow you to connect your efforts. As in many other sports there are five training methods, which Paul Köchli defines as follows:

- **Continuous training,** with a small stimulation intensity (minimum, light, or medium) without stopping. In continuous training in medium and light intensity, however, you should do segments lasting from 20 to 30 minutes and separate them with intervals of recuperation, especially during a long training ride on the road.

- **Repeat training,** which consists of a high number of efforts of short duration at a great intensity (high, submaximum, or maximum) with intervals of complete recuperation between them. The recuperation is evaluated by the heart rate which should drop to at least half its maximum rate, to around 90 to 100 beats per minute.

- **Interval training,** identical to the preceding one but with one important difference. The recuperation between two intervals is not complete. The heart rate only drops to 65% of maximum, or about 120 to 130 beats per minute.

- **Alternate training,** during which there is a continuous effort, but where intensity and duration are programmed beforehand—for example: 3 minutes at high intensity, 8 minutes at minimum intensity, 3 minutes at high intensity, 8 minutes at minimum intensity, 3 minutes at high intensity, etc.

- **Race simulation,** which imitates the efforts required in competition according to the terrain and other characteristics of the ride. It's what often happens during a group ride when somebody really blasts off in the last kilometers.

All these forms of training are useful, especially interval training which develops power, in the usual sense of the word in bicycle racing. Knowing these categories and being able to apply them to yourself by using a watch, a heartrate monitor, or at least a speedometer should enable a serious amateur to train very effectively, working on all the qualities of a good racer with the main goal of improving his weaknesses.

However, if you're ambitious you need to have a qualified coach to set up a real training program with precise goals. He would also keep track of its effects on your fitness and on performance levels as you go along. The help of a sports doctor is also desirable for medical monitoring as well as for advice in defining the initial training programs on the basis of tests of your cardiac and metabolic capacities. This is how desirable thresholds of cardiac output are determined at the beginning of the training period. They can be readjusted as you progress.

Whatever the case, the bicycle racer would be well advised to develop his self-reliance for he's the one doing the pedaling. Even if his coach follows him in a car—which would only be in exceptional circumstances—the rider is the only one able to observe and analyze his sensations, just as in a race.

Current knowledge of sports physiology, the perfecting of training principles, and the technical means available make his task a lot easier, if he's willing to use them.

As for the enlightened amateur who rides for his own pleasure, he now has everything he needs to really enjoy himself on the road and to keep from harming himself by dangerous and inappropriate efforts.

The cyclist's physical qualities

The goal of cycling workouts and, more generally, of physical training techniques—gymnastics, weight training, stretching—is to develop the rider's physical capacities in two ways:

— to increase the duration of effort at the various intensity levels by developing the metabolic and cardiovascular capacities;

— to increase the efficiency of the movements used in all kinds of efforts by developing specific qualities of the various muscle groups which come into play.

These two areas are closely linked, for metabolism produces all the chemical and electrical reactions at the cellular level, especially in the muscles. These reactions determine the cyclist's physical qualities, on which performance directly depends.

The cyclist's general physical qualities are much the same as those of any athlete. According to Georges Lambert they are currently described as these six:

— *coordination*, attained by a series of muscle contractions and decontractions that are very precise in intensity and duration;

— *flexibility*, which provides a great range of motion;

— *strength*, a concept not as obvious as it appears if you compare it to the term as it's used in mechanics, because the "strength" of a muscle can't be isolated unless the movement that accompanies it is of minimum speed;

— *speed*, which includes the reaction time needed to get moving, the time needed to carry out an action, and the rapidity with which it is repeated;

— *power*, the ability to produce a great amount of muscular work in a relatively short period of time, from 30 seconds to several minutes;

— *endurance*, the ability to perform a task steadily for a long period of time.

In most sports the combinations of these different qualities also come into play:

— *endurance-strength*, well demonstrated in mountain climbing;

— *speed-strength*, used in sprints;

— *endurance-speed*, the prerogative of six-day riders;

— *speed-flexibility*, also shown by track riders and those who pedal "in butter," to use cycling jargon.

Paul Köchli has used similar concepts to define the characteristic qualities the cyclist needs to perform various kinds of activities in his own sport. He bases them on two simple and quantifiable ideas—strength intensity and movement intensity.

● **Endurance:** the racer is able to ride as long as possible at minimum stimulation intensity at a fairly low speed without pushing too hard on the pedals, assuming that he can stay in the saddle for hours at a time. Without this basic quality, which in a way justifies old-fashioned training, it's impossible to acquire good recuperative ability and to withstand a large workload at a higher level.

● **Critical endurance:** this is endurance brought to a higher degree of tempo and strength, up to the threshold of medium intensity but before reaching oxygen debt, as when riding the hour record on the track. The adjective "critical" speaks to the fact that the organism is already highly stressed.

● **Strength-power:** the cyclist rides as long as he can at submaximum, high, or medium stimulation intensity with great strength intensity and moderate movement intensity. Here are three examples:

• a long final sprint from the front, forcing the pace on short climbs not longer than 2 minutes, as well as attacks and counterattacks of the same length (closing or opening a gap) at submaximum stimulation intensity;

• prologue time trials no longer than 4 minutes, and the same examples as above for an equivalent length of time at high stimulation intensity;

• time trials no longer than a half hour and sustained efforts for the same length of time on a hill or on the flat at medium stimulation intensity.

• **Speed-power:** this time, in the same three areas of stimulation intensity as above (submaximum, high, and medium) the racer rides as long as possible with moderate strength intensity and great movement intensity, as in the following examples, given in decreasing order:
  • trying to regain a lap in a six-day chase (submaximum);
  • 3km pursuit, not counting the start (high);
  • 5km pursuit, not counting the start (medium).

• **Acceleration:** this is the quality that allows a cyclist to ride at maximum stimulation intensity, with the greatest strength intensity and very little movement intensity, as in standing starts on the track and on the road, and hard accelerations from a slow speed (especially on a hill), which are usually ridden out of the saddle.

• **Explosive strength:** at maximum stimulation intensity, the effort is very brief (10 to 25 seconds) and combines great strength intensity with great movement intensity. The final phases of a track sprint and of a road sprint when the rider jumps an opponent at the line are good examples of this, as is the 200m flying start on the track.

• **Velocity:** this quality is not a direct factor during competition, where you always need a minimum gear to go fast. But it highlights the coordination needed for pedaling and, together with muscular strength, develops the speed of the sprint. It is a question of riding at maximum stimulation intensity with the greatest possible movement intensity and very low strength intensity, by spinning. This is possible with a small gear on a false flat, on descents, or in flying starts.

Training programs

Training deserves a book all to itself and is open to infinite variations. It's impossible to draw up theoretical programs that would be suitable for everyone. You have to consider motivation, temperament, and actual situations on the road.

First of all, everything depends on fixed objectives and the fitness level at the start. Training principles remain the same, but their application varies according to whether the training is for a champion getting ready for a race, an amateur who hopes to turn pro, a sport rider who wants to improve his performance, or a tourist who suddenly decides he wants to train to compete in veterans' races.

That's why we don't give a standard program but just suggestions and some examples.

Winter training

For winter training, when there are no races, both amateur and professional riders maintain the minimum amount of activity to enable them to resume regular training in the best shape. Note that more specific training for professionals starts with the races at the beginning of February, so they have to stay in quite good shape. There used to be a more definite break in winter and extra pounds were more common at the time of the traditional return to training on the Côte d'Azur.

Winter training, as we define it, is recommended for all categories of riders, even beginners. For them it would be the best way to prepare for cycling, to have a body and an organism capable of getting through their first season in good style. The only difference for beginners would be that they wouldn't ride cyclocross or track in the winter and perhaps wouldn't do any weight training unless they were very motivated.

Winter training takes advantage of three kinds of disciplines:

— body maintenance and development activities, such as gymnastics, weight training, and stretching;

— other sports offering the cyclist, who is often too specialized in his own area, the chance to develop his flexibility, dexterity, sense of balance, muscular tone, and cardiovascular capacity;

— winter riding, including cyclocross and track cycling.

Everyone should establish an appropriately individualized program of body development. This will be the subject of a later section.

As for other sports, there are lots of them and you can give your imagination free rein. Here are the principal ones:

● **Running** is a sport you can do any time, any place, and this is not an unimportant advantage. Wooded areas are best. Running stengthens the ankles, which are only used in one plane when pedaling and therefore are vulnerable. It makes the arms and shoulders more supple—they suffer from the same problem. Finally, it helps to maintain and increase cardiovascular capacity. For the first weeks it's useless to work on anything but endurance. After that, be careful of too violent accelerations. They might cause a pulled muscle, especially in the calf area where the muscles get very specialized from cycling. Running combines very well with flexibility exercises, which then get the benefit of being done in the fresh air. Runs should be progressively increased up to an hour and a half. Begin with about 10 minutes of warm-up.

• **Swimming** is highly recommended because it's complementary to cycling, though it should be avoided during the competition period. It develops the rib cage and the respiratory capacities. But above all it strengthens the muscles around the spine. Swimming on your back is especially beneficial because the spinal column is stretched out without accentuating its curvature the way the breast stroke does.

• **Crosscountry skiing** is the cyclist's favorite winter sport. The endurance sport *par excellence*, it provides very good basic conditioning. It's done in the mountains at a medium altitude in very clean air. The workouts can be long and not very intense in the beginning, then shorter and more sustained later on. Crosscountry skiing makes the arms and shoulders more supple and strengthens them. The work done by the lower limbs is a very good preparation for pedaling—especially lifting the back foot, which you should concentrate on practicing. In addition, cross-country skiing develops your sense of balance.

• **Skating** is a somewhat unknown sport which cyclists should do more often. It develops the thigh, lumbar, and abdominal muscles in a position which resembles that of a rider on the drops. There's no contact point for the arms, so the back has to get stronger. Be sure your spinal column is in good shape because skating can reveal weaknesses.

• **Team sports** like football, handball, volleyball, and basketball shouldn't be ignored. They allow the cyclist to cultivate his reflexes and dexterity and to practice changes of tempo. But watch out for possible injuries and pulled muscles, particularly on artificial turf.

Cyclocross and track cycling are both favored by cyclists in the offseason.

● **Cyclocross** is a very demanding sport if you want good results. It requires physical fitness that would be difficult for a rider to acquire if he wants to race a complete road season. At least partial recuperation is a psychological and physiological necessity in winter. There are many road riders who race cyclocross once a week or more to keep in minimum shape while improving their dexterity and flexibility on the bike.

● **Track riding** has other followers and provides the advantage of developing qualities such as dexterity, flexibility, and especially speed. The evenness of the track rider's pedal stroke offers a useful complement to the road rider who sometimes gets too used to pushing, especially since the advent of big gears.

Training on the bicycle

Only those riders who are preparing for a particular goal need a real training plan spread out over several weeks. Each session is determined by the chosen training method, its duration, and the stimulation intensity. The best example is when Francesco Moser trained for three months for the hour record at the beginning of '84. To a lesser degree we could cite Jacques Anquetil, who withdrew to his home in Normandy for three weeks to train for the Grand Prix of Nations. He won this queen of time trial events nine times in nine attempts. An absolute record. Most of the time training proceeds from day to day in order to acquire and maintain the best possible fitness.

A well thought-out training program depends on several fairly simple principles.

How to measure maximum heart rate

*T*he intensity ranges correspond to heartrate thresholds which are expressed as a percentage of maximum heart rate:
— *minimum intensity, from 65 to 80% of MHR;*
— *light intensity, from 80 to 90% of MHR;*

— medium intensity, from 90 to 100% of MHR.
There are two ways of measuring maximum heart rate:

● Tests on bicycle ergometers

This kind of test also allows you to measure maximum oxygen uptake and to make an electrocardiogram of your effort. From this you can learn how your heart is functioning and detect possible abnormalities.

The drawback of this procedure is that it puts the subject in an artificial situation, very different from that encountered on the road. Cardiovascular functioning is especially stimulated by the thermal regulation process. In the absence of all ventilation the organism gets rid of heat by opening the capillaries—even the peripheral ones—to the maximum. The effect is somewhat similar to a sauna. A significant part of cardiac reaction is due to thermal regulation and not to the metabolic load demanded by the effort. This makes the results deceptive.

● Measuring on the road

Measuring the heart rate on the road requires a cardiac watch. Best results are obtained by the "Sport-tester" type which registers the number of beats every 5, 15, or 60 seconds according to your choice. It can display the curve if you use the related electronic equipment. But the watch alone is amply sufficient for a good measurement. This is the method recommended by Paul Köchli.

Pick out a long hill that takes at least seven minutes to climb —it's an indication of size. After a preliminary warm-up, ride for five minutes at "critical" intensity, at the line between light and medium intensity where the organism is getting ready to partially use anaerobic metabolism. At this intensity you can still control your breathing, but just barely. At the end of these five minutes the body is ready to change its way of functioning. You must accelerate by alternating the seated and out-of-the-saddle positions so that you "blow up" at the end of three minutes. This way you can be sure of reaching high intensity, because your body has produced enough lactic acid to put your cardiovascular system into a situation of total effort. Heart rate is then at its maximum, and you just read it on the watch.

• The principle of overloading

Intensity, frequency, and duration are what determine the progressive overloading which helps the rider increase his capacities over the weeks. Intensity is the most important factor for a high-level rider because it's linked to the development of maximum aerobic strength, called VO_2 max. It's the work done at increasing intensity that makes all the difference between a racer and a tourist.

The duration and frequency of the training sessions—without forgetting time for total or partial recuperation—make it possible for the individual to shape his training according to his existing fitness level.

• The principle of workload compatibility

Riders used to enter their training mileage in notebooks.

This information is useful as long as you know how the distance was covered. During the season, 50 flat-out kilometers are more effective than 100 km at a leisurely pace.

The concept of "load" has an important precision. Load measures the amount of energy used in a training session.

Paul Köchli's method is to use a numerical score to evaluate the amount of load furnished during a session. This score is calculated by multiplying the length of the session in hours by the stimulation intensity expressed as an integer representing the percent of maximum intensity.

Here again are the average coefficients used:

minimum intensity . . .30
light intensity . . .45
medium intensity . . .55
high intensity . . .65
submaximum intensity . . .80
maximum intensity . . .95

Thus, one and a half hours of training at minimum intensity would read as: $1.5 \times 30 = 45$.

When an interval training session consists of 6 repeats of 1 minute each at submaximum intensity, separated by recovery periods of about 3 minutes, it lasts approximately half an hour. The numerical score of such a session would be equal to: $0.5 \times 80 = 40$. Recuperation periods actually count in the load period because the organism is carrying out important metabolic work which is part of training. There is a pause in stimulation but not a pause in load. This makes calculating easier because you're counting the total time without having to go into details.

And from here, if you make a note every day of the numerical score of the work done, a bit of addition will give you the week's total, which tells you more precisely about your amount of training.

With a little practice you can even evaluate the work done in a race. If you sit on wheels the whole time you'll stay at minimum intensity. If you break away for 40 km you can add an hour or so of light intensity. A lively race poses more difficult problems of evaluation but this doesn't matter. What counts is the principle of the method. The calculations are not an end in themselves and an approximation is enough.

A professional rider in the competition period reaches a numerical score of 1,100 to 1,200 per week. He can even reach 1,400 in a stage race at its most rigorous and 1,200 in a six-day. Sometimes decried as a sports media event, six-days demand a great deal from riders.

Someone beginning training is capable of 300 per week.

You are probably somewhere between these two extremes.

Be assured, in any case, that your threshold of workload compatibility, which you should try not to exceed by too much, depends on your training level as a cyclist. It will rise regularly as your fitness does.

The quick calculations above will help you find your threshold.

• The principle of cycles

Like life, training is governed by cycles of various sizes.

L. Matviev, a Soviet training specialist of some authority, describes a whole series of cycles which affect the progressive increase of training workload, the only guarantee of improved performance.

A single training session already constitutes a little cycle of effort/recovery. If you think of interval training you'll see mini-cycles of effort and partial recovery within the session itself.

Paul Köchli first defines a very variable cycle lasting anywhere from 9 to 30 weeks and made up of three periods: preparation, competition, and transition, lasting approximately 45%, 45%, and 10% of the total.

Each of these periods is composed of one or several macrocycles of 3 to 7 weeks which end with a recovery phase of several days. Each of these macrocycles is composed of several microcycles of 3 to 7 days which end with one day of recovery.

Finally, each of these microcycles has one or two workouts daily, commonly called "training sessions."

In a well-designed training program the training sessions vary from one day to the next within each microcycle. The structure of the microcycle varies in turn within the macrocycles, which themselves vary according to whether it's the preparation, competition, or transition period.

Setting up such a program only makes sense for a competitor and should be done with the coach.

We'll only give a few principles to serve as a guide:

• Periods

— In the preparation period the main goal is to develop the workload compatibility by increasing the load while using up energy reserves. You must increase your aerobic capacity with very long load duration and small intensities.

— In the competition period the goal is to reach peak form. So you must not exhaust your energy reserves in training but develop anaerobic capacity with high intensities and small durations.

— In the transition period very small quantities of work—always aerobic—allow you to recuperate.

• Macrocycles

— In basic training, which concerns all amateurs and non-professional racers, there will be especially long macrocycles. Short macrocycles, of 3 weeks for example, are only useful for top riders.

— The distinction between a preparation macrocycle and a competition macrocycle is a bit of a formal one. The difference is mostly in the degree of fitness. The preparation macrocycle can very easily include some competition, in the literal sense, which will help raise the fitness level. For example, a small stage race could end a preparation macrocycle.

— The preparation macrocycle should lead to total exhaustion of the energy resources. The competition macrocycle, on the contrary, should avoid that. It is well known that an athlete who is in shape should maintain and refine his fitness but doesn't need to work as hard as he did in the period when he was acquiring it.

— Intensity is highest, on the average, in the competition macrocycle and decreases quite dramatically from beginning to end. Intensity is lower at the start and grows during the preparation macrocycle, at least during the first part of the cycle.

• Microcycles

— Whatever their length, microcycles are characterized by a progressive increase in the amount of load and a decrease in intensity.

— The starting intensity is relative to the fitness level obtained during the previous macrocycle.

• Example of a typical chart

Group training, in a club, lends itself well to a weekly program of two microcycles—one from Tuesday to Friday, the other from Saturday to Monday—as in the chart below.

At the start of the microcycle you would work on velocity, explosive strength, acceleration, and speed-power and strength-power at the upper intensity levels (exacting technique, high intensity, short duration).

At the end of the cycle you would work on speed-power and strength-power at the lower intensity levels, critical endurance, and endurance (less exacting technique, small intensity, great duration).

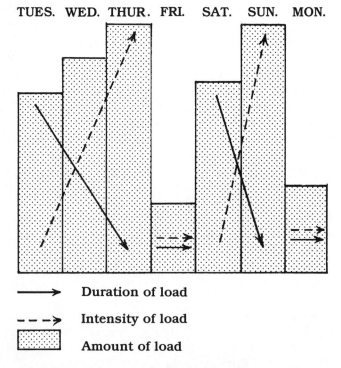

TUES. WED. THUR. FRI.   SAT.   SUN.   MON.

⟶   **Duration of load**

- - -➤   **Intensity of load**

▨   **Amount of load**

An example of a microcycle during the week

On the recovery day—called active rest—you would only work aerobically at minimum and light intensities for short durations.

body maintenance and development

Bicycle racing used to get a rather bad press from physical education instructors because it is not a "natural" sport. To listen to them, you would think the bicycle racer would overdevelop some muscles to the detriment of others—all in the legs, nothing in the arms—and would force his body into positions detrimental to its growth. He would be condemned to a rounded back, a skimpy chest, a soft stomach, and spindly arms. This pessimistic image has been largely contradicted by the well-balanced and athletic build that a great number of bike racers have today.

Besides, any sport practiced in large doses has its drawbacks that lead to a specific pathology, and each one proves to be artificial in some way.

It's been a long time since Biagio Cavanna, Fausto Coppi's blind soigneur, forbade his champion to even go hiking and recommended that he sleep in a hunting dog's position to keep a posture close to the one he used on the bike.

Today gymnastics, weight training, and stretching—to mention only the major disciplines—give the cyclist a way to compensate for the effects of body positions required by his sport. They are also a way to develop qualities useful in his own discipline and to work on weak points.

On a bicycle—and not just in the mountains—any useless weight is a handicap, even if it's muscles and not fat. Shoulders and arms like a weight lifter's are a disadvantage, including aerodynamically because the rider's frontal area increases.

You must have an athlete's body without being a body-builder. The knight in the Middle Ages had to have himself hoisted on to his horse because of the stiffness and weight of his armor. This shouldn't be true of the cyclist as he mounts his bicycle.

His body should allow him to act and react in a dynamic way in all circumstances and in the most varied positions—especially when pedaling out of the saddle. This assumes that all his muscles are sufficiently developed, that he remains supple, and that he has worked on his range of motion. All these qualities would be useful in case of a fall.

Moreover, the best results in pedaling come if the joints function as freely as possible, with a range greater than what you see while the movement is actually performed. For example, a rider in whom the muscles used to lift the thigh to the pelvis are well developed will be able to raise the knee to the upper dead spot more easily, even in a low position. He will also pedal more efficiently.

Maintaining a riding position with the torso horizontal shouldn't restrict pedal action. We are referring to the hamstring muscles which have a tendency to shorten from pedaling. As opposing muscles they can interfere with the raising of the thigh by exerting an undesirable pull on the pelvis.

Stretching the hamstrings is a remedy, as the Japanese sprinters have so often demonstrated at competitions.

These two examples show the importance of body development as a complement to more specific cycling training.

Here are some objectives, among others;

— to develop the quality and mass of the muscles used continuously in pedaling;

— to develop other muscles that are used less often but are occasionally necessary—for example, when riding out of the saddle;

— to strengthen the muscles used in static contraction to maintain your riding position;

— to make your entire body more supple and allow it to work in a relaxed way, since any tension during effort—whether static or dynamic—consumes energy.

Some riders have a poor riding position because they lack the body flexibility needed to find the best posture on their bike. They should try to correct this, as far as their physique allows, by doing appropriate exercises.

Finally, exercising the body helps maintain your fitness because it also works the cardiovascular system. As such, these disciplines are a part of winter training, a period where the cyclist rides much less. The winter break—less pronounced than it used to be but still necessary, if only psychologically—is thus balanced by maintaining a good physiological functioning.

Gymnastics

Gymnastics, calisthenics, and physical education are beneficial. So are those other activities based on a series of "natural" exercises whose purpose is to compensate for civilized man's progressively dwindling physical activity, caused by the conditions of his life.

These exercises focus on several goals:
— strengthening muscles which are not ordinarily used;
— making the body more flexible, through stretching;
— improving respiratory capacity, by opening the rib cage;
— working the cardiovascular system.

Gymnastics is an invaluable complement to cycling and can eliminate some of the stiffness that comes from practicing cycling exclusively.

It's done without equipment, or at most with small dumbbells or with weights on your ankles. This lets you work it in with an outdoor running session, alone or in a group.

Gymnastic or calisthenic workouts lasting about half an hour can be performed in an ordinary room, preferably with the window open, or in a specialized center. In the latter case, using a treadmill with adjustable resistance can replace running for the preliminary warm-up. It stimulates the respiratory and particularly the cardiovascular systems. Jumping rope can fulfill this role also. We will not give a typical program here. On one hand, these exercises are known by all. On the other, we believe that it's better to set up a program with a specialized professional. He'll identify weak points that need particular work and draw attention to movements that should be avoided in some individual instances and to necessary precautions about carrying out a motion.

Generally, you would work on:
— the abdominal muscles, which help in breathing and in the proper functioning of the digestive organs, and which contribute to the support of the spinal column;
— the lumbar and dorsal muscles, which allow you to maintain a stretched-out position, stabilize the pelvis on the saddle, and help pedaling while out of the saddle;
— the hip flexors, which raise the thigh, a basic pedaling movement. This movement, if not done well, can impede lifting the pedal and passing strongly through the upper dead spot. It's even more crucial in a low position, where the thigh angle is reduced;
— the hamstrings, stretching them to avoid the shortening which would be detrimental to flexibility and regular pedaling;
— the muscles which open the rib cage, to increase respiratory capacity and to help control breathing.

We speak of muscles for the sake of simplicity. In reality all the components of the locomotor system benefit from gymnastics—

tendons, ligaments, joint cartilage—and even the bones, whose blood vessels multiply when they are regularly stressed. This is why fractures heal more readily in athletes than they do in people who are not active.

Traditional gymnastics focuses simultaneously on flexibility, stretching, and strengthening the muscles. Two other disciplines have appeared more recently with more specific goals. One, weight training, aims to develop muscular strength. The other, stretching, works more systematically in that area.

We will examine them in that order.

Weight training

Once based almost exclusively on the use of dumbbells and barbells, weight training techniques are now very diversified. Today weight training relies more and more on sophisticated machinery which enables you to vary the kinds of work required of the muscle.

As its name implies, weight training is the development of the musculature, not to be confused with body building. Muscle size itself is not a goal. You are trying to improve the physiological and dynamic properties of the muscle by submitting it to increasing and controlled loads, something which specialized training for a particular sport doesn't provide.

No sport, whatever it may be, ever puts a single muscle to work, but rather muscle groups which are flexed and relaxed in turn as successive movements are performed.

The loads put on the muscles can vary from one set to another, but within fairly small limits.

Weight training is a technique which allows you to work a muscle—more often a muscle group—by isolating the others. With a precise result in mind, the elaborate variations are infinite in number. They can combine criteria such as the form of resistance, the degree of resistance, the method of contraction, the number of exercises, the number of sets for each exercise, the number of repetitions for each set, the length of rest between sets, the tempo of the workout, and many others.

With a well-designed program you can lengthen or shorten a muscle, increase or decrease its tone, adapt it for static or dynamic work, and develop its capacity for strength, endurance, speed, and power.

Weight training thus turns an athlete into a sorcerer's apprentice if he's working blindly. This is why the cyclist should under no circumstances plunge into weight training without getting the advice and following the recommendations of a qualified coach who is familiar with both weight training and cycling.

Weight training alone in a room equipped with the necessary machinery without having a clear idea of what you are undertaking can lead to disappointment and cause results which are the opposite of what you wanted. A sprinter, proud to be able to lift larger and larger weights and satisfied to note an increase in the circumference of his thigh, might well lose his kick.

Besides this, the risk of injury is not negligible, especially in the lumbar vertebrae area if you're using heavy weights indiscriminately.

The exercise program should be very precise—a little like the work done in high, submaximum, and maximum intensities on the bicycle—because serious weight training relies heavily on respiratory, cardiovascular, and metabolic functions. Breathing, especially, must be kept within the limits of the given program.

Once these precautions are taken, weight training during the winter provides a very good complementary training for the cyclist. It allows him to correct weak points and to develop specific qualities, especially his sprint, and to considerably strengthen his back.

With weight training the cyclist will get round a weakness of some muscles in the lower extremities—such as those of the thighs and the hamstrings—and will effectively tone the sacro-lumbar and abdominal groups.

Alex Pontet, former sprint champion and French national track coach, directs the weight training workouts of the young riders he's responsible for. He feels that a road rider should be very cautious about weight training for the legs. But he wholeheartedly recommends upper body work—that is, the back, the abdominal girdle, and not neglecting the rib cage and the shoulders. Road racing requires long hours in the saddle. This inhibits the expansion of the rib cage and immobilizes the shoulders. Weight training, even more than gymnastics, allows you to correct these effects. Alex Pontet also recommends following each weight training session by 10 minutes of stretching or 15 minutes on a stationary bike. This is essential for maintaining flexibility, keeping good coordination in pedaling, and avoiding any shortening of the muscles.

Stretching

The American riders on the La Vie Claire team do their stretching regularly, and not only because the word is Anglo-Saxon. They understand physiology well enough to understand its usefulness, and have integrated it into their daily routine.

Paul Köchli feels that the ideal would be to stretch at least once a day and, if possible, before and after a race or training session.

"Stretching" means the deliberate and reasoned practice of stretching. It has nothing to do with the repeated and mechanical stretching of ordinary gymnastics, done by rhythmic rocking of the leg or the arm to the farthest point. That kind of dynamic stretching does not put tension on the muscles, the main goal of stretching. Putting tension on the muscles lengthens them quickly and thus increases the range of motion of the joints.

The principle of stretching rests on the fact that if a muscle group makes a limb move quickly towards an extreme position it sends a signal to the central nervous system which calls the opposing muscles into play. These then attempt to slow down the movement in order to avoid torn fibers. This defense mechanism is very useful in everyday life, because it counteracts excessively wide movements which would threaten to disarticulate the skeleton. But because it contracts the opposing muscles and keeps them from stretching, it defeats the goal of the exercise.

This is why stretching is a kind of slow gymnastics. You must keep the neuro-muscular fuse from sending the signal to the muscle telling it to contract. Thus the muscle fibers, the connecting tissue fibers—which resist rapid contraction—and the tendons on both ends of the muscles are all stretched simultaneously. In stretching, you hold the extreme position for 30 seconds during which you seek to be conscious of what is happening, as in yoga.

Like weight training, stretching is a group of techniques which are very precise in detail and which we will not go into here. There are specialized books, but the best way is still to learn from a competent coach. Stretching just before a competition, like a time trial, prepares the muscles for the effort by making them more supple and increasing their tone. The alternating pattern of contraction-relaxation is more completely guaranteed, enhancing your effectiveness if you must ride fast and giving you a more efficient style if you must ride for a long time.

After the race a stretching session, even a short one, helps recuperation.

Among the very beneficial results of stretching we will mention the possibility of being able to raise your saddle and still be able to pedal with suppleness and retain good speed. You'll be able to do this because of an improved decontraction of the opposing muscles with each pedal revolution. The hamstrings which instinctively attempt to hold back the descending leg reap a great benefit from stretching. It is their imperfect decontraction that prevents you from raising the saddle enough. Remember that the advantage of a sufficiently high saddle is twofold. On the one hand, you get a superior ergonomic return. On the other, the spinal column is in a better position to resist the strains of cycling.

medical aspects of cycling

pathology of cycling

by Doctors Bernard Teboul and Jacques-Louis Rey

Every sport has its own pathology. Everyone has heard of "tennis elbow," an elbow condition named after tennis. Cycling is no exception to the rule.

After a brief discussion of specific problems of the lower limbs caused by pedaling, we will deal with the cyclist's most common medical problems.

The sequence of movements in the lower limbs

When we observe a working cyclist, his knee seems to be operating like a crankshaft mechanism.

However, the knee doesn't only work in the plane of flexion-extension. There is a second kind of mobility caused by the assymetry of the two femoral condyles. This automatically causes the tibia to rotate in relation to the femur with each movement of flexion-extension.

Two different things may happen during flexion-extension:

— if the foot isn't resting on anything, the tibia will turn in relation to the femur;

— if the foot is pressing on something, then the tibia can't turn and so the femur rotates in relation to the tibia.

Because his foot is attached to the pedal, the cyclist is an example of the second case. The tibia can no longer turn, and this leads to a small rotation of the femur with each flexion extension. In order not to restrict the femur's automatic rotation in relation to the tibia it is of utmost importance that the cyclist does controlled tests before settling on a definitive position of his shoes on the pedals. The rider must feel that his foot position on the pedal is such that the femur has the greatest freedom of movement. This isn't possible if the shoes are turned too much in either direction, and the results of such extreme positions are quickly felt. A poor foot position will hinder the femur's rotation in relation to the tibia and will naturally cause problems in and around the joints.

Indeed, the muscles of the pes anserinus in particular, but also the biceps femoris and tensor fascia lata, may be subject to abnormal tensions in trying to correct this bad position.

This is why a poor foot alignment on the pedal might encourage the development of tendinitis.

Unlike the knee, the cyclist's hip is under very little stress for the following reasons:

— cycling is basically performed in a sitting position, so the stress of body weight is greatly reduced;

— the hip is a joint with three planes of movement, and is extremely supple.

Chondromalacia of the patella

A few numbers will demonstrate the importance of the forces exerted on the knee and especially on a small bone called the patella, or kneecap, which fulfills a crucial function.

When flexing the knee 130 degrees the force on the patella is 260 kg. At 145 degrees the pressure reaches 420 kg. If a 20 kg weight is attached to the foot, the force on the patella is about 400 kg when the leg is flexed 45 degrees and can reach 900 kg at 90 degrees.

These forces are enormous.

The patella is an intermediary bone between the quadriceps— a very powerful muscle, especially in cyclists—and the patellar tendon which is very strong and inserts on the anterior tibial tuberosity.

The patella has two facets which articulate with the femoral trochlea. This is a groove at the end of the femur formed by two

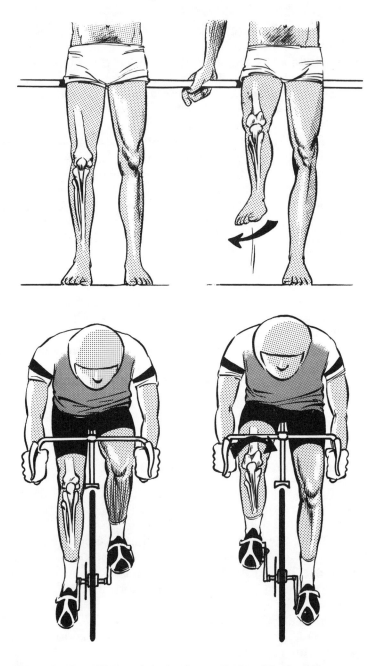

Top: When the foot is free and the leg flexes, it's the tibia that turns.

Bottom: With each revolution of the crank, the femur turns slightly in relation to the tibia because of the immobility of the foot on the pedal.

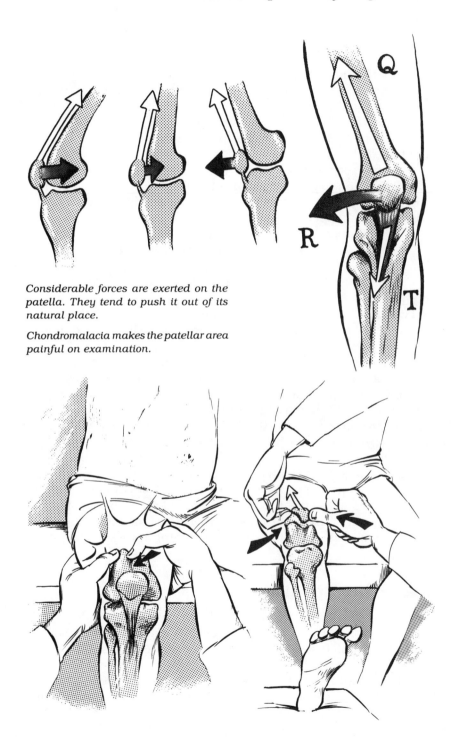

Considerable forces are exerted on the patella. They tend to push it out of its natural place.

Chondromalacia makes the patellar area painful on examination.

condyles which are exactly opposite each of the facets of the patella. It's very important to note that the lateral condyle is more prominent and its role is crucial.

The patella, which rides in the trochlea as if on a rail, is subjected to two forces:

— the force Q, from the quadriceps;

— the force T, which is the restraining force of the patellar tendon.

Since these two forces are not aligned, there is a resulting force R which tends to pull the patella out of the trochlea. Why doesn't the patella come out of its groove? There are many reasons why this doesn't happen:

— a strong posterior ridge on the patella holds it in place;

— the most medial fibers of the quadriceps are also very powerful;

— finally, and most importantly, the lateral condyle serves to restrain the patella.

Two conclusions must be highlighted here:

— the enormous stresses on the patella are well absorbed thanks to the presence of 8 to 10 mm of thick cartilage. The slightest contusion or attack on this cartilage results in immediate pain;

— since the balance of the patella is constantly threatened there is a danger of partially dislocating it. Abnormal stress resulting from this would then also lead to pain.

In either case we have the manifestation of a painful patello-femoral syndrome which is very difficult to treat. Cycling is then absolutely contraindicated. Indeed, cycling is a hard sport on the patella because it is required to work continuously.

These are a few reasons why the cyclist must pay special attention to the patellar mechanism and should see a specialist at the smallest sign of discomfort. Kinesitherapy plays a important role in the diagnosis and subsequent treatment of these patello-femoral problems.

Patellar tendinitis

A few numbers illustrate the problem.

During a foot race a force of 700 kg is exerted on the patellar tendon with each step. In certain circumstances these forces may be greater and reach 1,200 kg.

Patellar tendinitis is the name for the group of painful symptoms suffered by the patellar tendon. The cyclist puts special demands on this tendon because he pedals an average of 150 strokes per kilometer, or more than 30,000 in an average stage of the Tour de France.

The most common problem is insertion tendinitis which happens at the junction of the tendon and the bone. This junction is the site of micro-ruptures which have no opportunity to heal because of continuous and excessive demands. These micro-ruptures cause cysts and nodules that are sometimes fairly large. They lead to painful discomfort that can appear gradually or suddenly, following training or racing.

The pain is located in the patellar tendon and can become very intense when squatting. Squatting sometimes becomes impossible.

The treatment of patellar tendinitis is quite difficult.

Rest, along with physical therapy, ice packs, or fangotherapy (mud packs), may work in the beginning as long as the return to training is slow and gradual. If this fails, injections and immobilization in a knee cast can help control the pain. But in these cases the tendinitis often becomes chronic. Medical treatment has then failed.

Surgical intervention can be considered. It consists of "scraping" the patellar tendon. In this case the return to physical activity may be long—from four to six months.

Achilles tendinitis

The Achilles tendon is the most powerful tendon in the body. In experimental studies on corpses, the tendon resists forces greater than 300 kg before breaking. In a living person the Achilles tendon is probably able to sustain much greater stress.

The Achilles tendon is an essential element in serious cycling because it allows the athlete to transmit all his energy with each pedal stroke. Continuous demand on this tendon can be the source of feared tendinitis.

There are many causes of this tendinitis. We will mention the major ones:

— the Achilles tendon is surrounded by bursae which allow the tendon to slide smoothly on surrounding tissue. These bursae can be irritated and become a source of pain (bursitis);

— the Achilles tendon is surrounded by a protective synovial sleeve. This sleeve can itself be the site of a painful inflammation;

— the tendon itself may be injured:

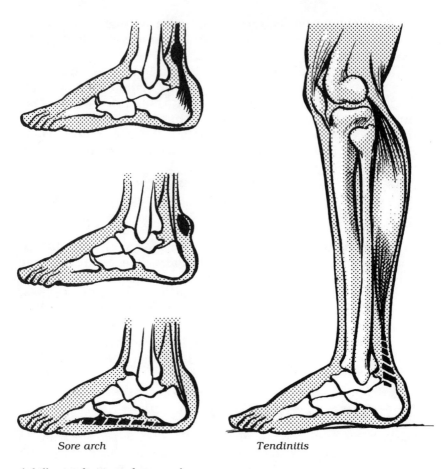

Sore arch   Tendinitis

Achilles tendinitis and sore arch

● the body of the tendon is sometimes the site of micro-ruptures. If these can't heal they sometimes lead to extensive and often painful nodules;

● the insertion of the tendon at the calcaneus (heel bone) can also be the site of micro-ruptures, which are painful too. This is calcaneal enthesitis.

● finally, there can be partial or even total rupture of the tendon, sometimes even during very slight effort.

Rest is the main characteristic of the treatment of Achilles tendinitis.

Anti-inflammatories, physical therapy, injections, or even a cast may prove sufficient. Only if these fail will surgical intervention be considered.

Pes anserinus tendinitis

Three muscles insert on the medial face of the upper end of the tibia—the sartorius, the semitendinosus, and the gracilis—and are collectively called the pes anserinus muscles.

These three muscles end in a tendon group which slides on the medial surface of the top of the tibia for about 6 to 10 centimeters before it inserts.

Between these tendons and the tibia there is a very important bursa which allows the tendons to slide without chafing on the bone.

Remember that this group of muscles has two functions, that of bending the knee and that of assisting the internal rotation of the tibia in relation to the femur.

This bursa can become inflamed when it's subjected to too much stress, either because of bad shoe position on the pedal or because

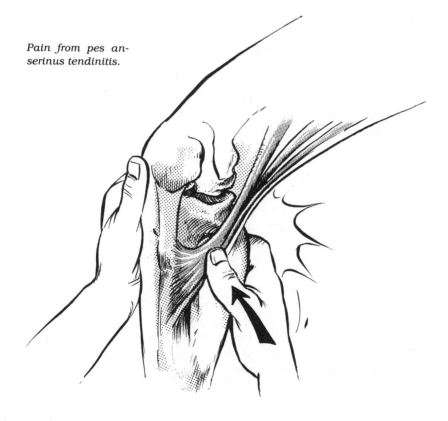

Pain from pes anserinus tendinitis.

the muscles remain contracted instead of relaxing. In the latter case they work against the powerful quadriceps. Pain is then felt and it gets worse as the pedaling becomes more and more uneven. This starts a viscious circle which promotes the development of tendino-bursitis.

Treatment is then difficult. Physiotherapy and rest may still be effective. If not, surgery must be considered.

Treating tendinitis

Treating tendinitis is not very easy. When detected early enough, rest plus physical therapy, ice, or fangotherapy may be effective.

— The rest period must be substantial, at least three to five weeks and even up to three months, before considering surgical intervention.

— Applying ice packs a few times a day for 20 minutes has a double effect. It reduces the inflammation and numbs the superficial pain. Using ice can lead to a definite improvement in combination with the application of heavy layers of anti-inflammatory cream at night. This form of treatment does not exclude others and can be combined with physical therapy or an appropriate kinesitherapy.

— Physical therapy, which includes electric treatments, is used to reduce pain and fight inflammation, and this reduces swelling. The main electric currents used are low frequency, middle frequency, and continuous. The latter includes "ionopherese." The principle of ionopherese is to introduce healing ions in the bruised area. Ultrasound, short-wave, and, more rarely, radiotherapy are also used.

— Fangotherapy, or treatment by applying hot mud packs, requires a special procedure and should be left to experts.

— Splints may be used during the night.

— Casts can totally immobilize the problem area for a given length of time.

— A heel splint is useful in Achilles tendinitis to reduce stress on the tendon and thereby give it more rest.

These treatments can be combined with a medical prescription of anti-inflammatory drugs, analgesics, and muscle relaxants.

The return to training must be slow and gradual. It's essential that it be combined with appropriate rehabilitation as well as observation of the rider in action on the road.

General prevention of tendinitis

Here we will review the principal causes of tendinitis. The elimination of these causes is the basis of prevention.

— nutritional mistakes should not be overlooked. For the prevention of tendinitis we particularly stress the importance of the carbohydrate ration and of a balanced protein intake—that is, not too much;

— some diseases may favor the occurrence of tendinitis, such as:

- dental diseases;
- hypercholesterolemia;
- hyperuricemia (gout).

— some morphological types are more prone to tendinitis than others. In particular, people with high arches often also have a shorter Achilles tendon and this can be a cause of tendinitis;

— after any trauma, regardless of its nature, the return to physical activity must be closely monitored, especially in highly trained athletes. In some cases there is a lack of coordination in the beginning, and this can lead to tendinitis or worsen a pre-existing condition.

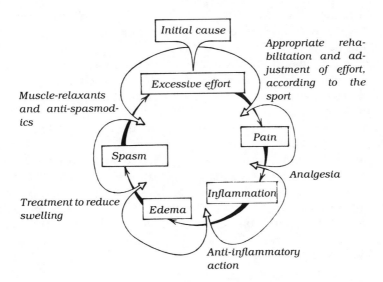

The vicious circle of tendinitis, with appropriate attempts to interrupt it at each of its stages.

— a poorly conceived training program or an inadequate one can also lead to problems. A few important points must be remembered:

- it's very important to warm up and stretch the muscles before every training session and before every competition;
- in any sport one should avoid abrupt changes in the rhythm of the training program. Everything must be accomplished gradually;
- for the cyclist in particular, it's important to have a good knowledge of the muscles that contract successively with each pedal revolution, and to check that there is no abnormal functioning between opposing muscle groups;
- the adjustments of the bicycle must be carefully controlled by the coach. A saddle at the wrong height, handlebars that are too high, or a poorly positioned cleat are often the explanations and the main cause of a problem.

Foot pain

The large tuberosity of the calcaneus lies between two groups of tendons:

— proximally, the Achilles tendon;
— distally, the insertion of the muscles of the plantar arch.

This area of the calcaneus is therefore subjected to intense forces pulling in opposite directions.

The repeated and intense efforts produced in pedaling may lead to micro-traumas that may cause pericalcanear tendinitis.

When the problem occurs at the insertion of the Achilles tendon we have calcaneal enthesitis which we mentioned earlier.

Elsewhere, it could be tendinitis of the insertion of the muscles of the plantar arch.

Pain and discomfort often occur suddenly and it becomes very difficult to pedal. The treatment of tendinitis of the foot relies on physical therapy, which, when combined with fangotherapy and electrotherapy, is generally effective. If this fails, injections and cortisone treatments may be helpful. Orthopedic soles generally have only a temporary effect. Surgery is not recommended either and should only be considered as a last resort.

Pulled hamstrings

The hamstrings are powerful muscles starting at the ischium and ending at the knee. These muscles work to extend the hip and flex the knee.

In theory, when the hamstrings contract the quadriceps must relax. This sequence of contraction is particularly crucial for the cyclist.

If these two muscle groups contract simultaneously for some reason, the quadriceps, which is by far the more powerful of the two, will forcefully stretch the hamstrings, risking the tear of one or more groups of muscle fibers.

When such a pull or strain occurs it doesn't usually interrupt the effort immediately. It's only four to six hours later that pain appears. In cases of a severe pull, pain can be felt earlier and pedaling can become absolutely impossible after half an hour.

The treatment of a strained hamstring muscle consists primarily of rest. In a moderate case, the symptoms diminish rapidly and disappear after 10 to 14 days. In the case of a severe pull, however, pain may be slow to subside and may persist many weeks if not months. In either case, the return to racing must be slow and gradual. If pain reappears you must know how to reduce, and perhaps even stop, training.

Lower back pain

The junction between the trunk and the pelvis is constantly subjected to great stress in cycling.

It is well known that the lumbo-sacral joint is a susceptible region in human anatomy.

In the cyclist, this region is submitted to two types of stresses:
— road shock, intensified by the speed, particularly increases the pressure on the L5-S1 and L4-L5 disks;
— irregular or abnormal contraction of the paraspinous muscles.

When spinning is not smooth and regular, the cyclist puts excessive demands on the lumbo-sacral muscles which in turn subject the lumbo-sacral joint to extreme and abnormal stress. This explains the occurrence of lower back pain, which is sometimes worsened by a sciatic condition.

We think that a fluid riding style, putting the paraspinous muscles under the least possible stress, is most important for the cyclist.

How the rider rests his arms on the handlebars is fundamental. The flatter the trunk—that is, in a horizontal position—the less stress there will be on the lower spine which is then forced to straighten out. Obviously this flat position has a limit, because the knees still have to be able to go up and down.

A good way to achieve this position is to raise the saddle as

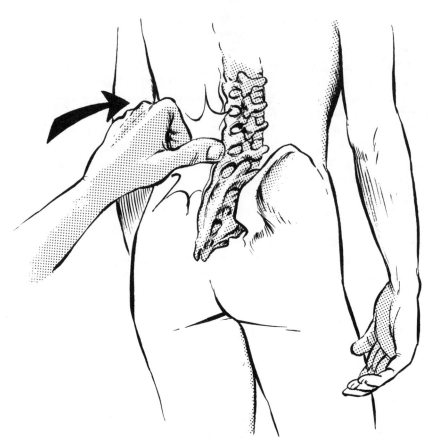

Localizing lower back pains

much as possible so that the body dives toward the bars. Of course, the distance between the saddle and the bars must be carefully adapted to each rider's morphological type.

By taking these steps the rider can avoid or at least diminish the severity and frequency of lower back pain. If it occurs despite these measures, a complete spinal examination is called for.

The treatment of lower back pain and sciatica is sometimes long and difficult.

First of all, an X-ray examination will look for a possible spinal anomaly.

Muscular spasm is a sign of all minor, acute, or chronic disturbances of the musculo-skeletal system. It signals a painful muscle reaction caused by a minor or major irritation of the joints, bones, spine, ligaments, or tendons. The result of this spasm is restricted movement, either because the spasm works against the desired movement or because it's painful.

As with tendinitis, you should always have the concept of the "vicious circle" in mind and know at which point to act. Corrective action will be different if the problem arises from a minor mechanical disorder or from an inflammation of purely muscular, ligamentous, or capsular origin.

If the problem is mechanical, the first step is to manipulate the injured section to readjust it and regain mobility. The second step includes the use of traction in combination with massage, fangotherapy, or physical therapy.

Rehabilitation then begins and can be myotensive, isometric, or proprioceptive. You can also try to improve your posture through autoelongation and segmental mobilization exercises.

After radiological examination, you can turn to orthopedic insoles for rebalancing or correction.

If the problem is caused by inflammation, you must attack it directly by electrotherapy, fangotherapy, massage, and traction. When improvement begins you can go on to an appropriate rehabilitation.

In both cases, and depending on the amount of pain, rest is supplemented by a medical treatment with anti-inflammatory drugs, analgesics, and muscle relaxants.

Local injections sometimes produce good results.

Should the previously mentioned therapies fail, a lumbo-spinal brace can be tried temporarily.

However, lower back pain associated with pain in the lower limbs might indicate the possibility of a herniated disk. The treatment is then more complex. The combination of manipulation and aggressive anti-inflammatory treatment may not be sufficient, in which case surgical intervention must be considered and may be necessary.

The elbow

Cyclists put great stress on their elbows, which function as shock absorbers between the wrist and the shoulder. So it isn't surprising that riders sometimes complain of elbow pain. Long rides can cause these pains to become chronic. Pressing on the olecranon during examination will cause a sharp pain. X-rays of the elbow may show a bone spur. Physiotherapy is generally sucessful in reducing this pain. However, if pain persists, surgical removal of this spur must be undertaken, and the results are usually good.

These varied examples clearly show the importance of proper choice of equipment and proper adjustment in order to cycle without getting injured.

The human body must function perfectly. The bicycle must be in good mechanical condition. But it is in their mutual relationship that the secret of cycling lies.

A team that includes a coach, a doctor, and a technician probably will contain all necessary skills.

medical follow-up

A physical exam is recommended at least once a year to check your general state of health.

This shouldn't, however, be just another routine visit to remeasure your weight, height, chest circumference, and other similar details.

A general practitioner can make sure your body is working properly from a functional point of view, but it's better to see a sports medicine specialist who knows cycling.

Beyond the general exam there are two interesting areas that can be further studied:

— analyzing cardio-respiratory functioning by a battery of tests which help evaluate the subject's athletic capabilities. These include electrocardiograms (at rest, during activity, and recuperating) and stress tests which measure, among other things, maximum oxygen consumption (VO_2 max), the heart rate that corresponds to the start of anaerobic metabolism, and maximal heart rate;

— biological analyses which monitor the body's functioning in the area of cellular metabolism, malnutrition, and possible deficiencies, especially in minerals. Blood analysis (cholesterol, sugar level, fat percent, uric acid) is indispensable in evaluating nutrition quality.

On one hand, these detailed tests provide reliable data on which to build a good training program. On the other hand, they help the athlete adapt his often inappropriate diet to bring him the nutrients he might be needing. Since every human being is different in these areas, it's important to get to know yourself in order to avoid blindly applying general rules. An evaluation should be done at least twice a year, once at the beginning of training, and later during the racing season.

A dental check-up is essential. Dental infection can be responsible for fatigue and poor performance, and may play havoc with the best training plans. These infections must be detected before they begin to affect your health.

Finally, it's clear that the collaboration of sports doctor, coach, and cyclist provides the best guarantee of health and success.

what cycling has done for me

by Bernard Hinault

Cycling has given me a lot of pleasure and continues to do so as I stand on the threshold of my last season. I enjoy training and racing. For me it's like a game.

It may sound surprising, but I have always thought of cycling as a game, even if it hurt my legs once in a while.

I'm often seeking a victory, but I also enjoy making things happen, no matter what the outcome.

I have included my teammates in this game. That is how a good team is formed. You shouldn't always hog the whole blanket to yourself.

I don't live like a monk. I take pleasure in life and I know how to live it fully. I work very hard; no task discourages me. But if I feel like having fun I don't hesitate, even in the middle of the season. It's good for the head. It's a matter of how much and of being organized.

Why bicycling and not some other sport? The question never came up for me. Everything fell into place quite naturally.

Cycling has given me the good fortune to live in the open air and to train on all kinds of terrain, from the plains to the mountain passes. No other sport offers the same opportunities, and this suits me very well. After all the years I've spent cranking out the miles in the pack I still take pleasure in the countryside as it rolls by and I always look at it, even in the toughest moments.

Cycling is a very demanding sport.

Through it I've been able to express myself completely, by giving the best of myself, sometimes to my utter limits. The intensity of the effort often helped to externalize a problem I found difficult to resolve. When not competing, I can't unwind on my bicycle the way everyone else does, but I do love to go on excursions. The mere act of keeping my balance on two wheels provides a certain distraction, especially on my mountain bike in the woods, off the beaten paths.

And the cycling world? Like all worlds, it has its good and bad aspects. It's important to go along with the good.

My success in cycling has allowed me to meet a large number of the famous from other worlds: athletes, artists, doctors, engineers, and businessmen.

I have always continued to learn from my contact with them, and it's not over yet!

a bicycle in my heart

by Claude Genzling

Ten years old: unexpected mastery of a new kind of equilibrium on an old bicycle scavenged from an attic. Entire days spent riding. Warm air flushes my cheeks. The streets of my village climb, descend, and turn endlessly in the summer light. Past the last houses, short breakaways in the midst of the fields.

Thirteen years old: flights and forays in the hollows of the Vosges mountains, from one valley to another, with a snack on my luggage rack. Endless downhills toward the plain which lies crushed under the August heat. Lemonade stops in the bistros around the empty village squares. Stocking up on fresh water, my forehead dripping with sweat, over the moss-covered troughs where the cows come to drink when the sun goes down. Long childhood reveries, ear cocked for the splash of a waterfall under the pines, my heart intoxicated by the brisk air. A verdant paradise recalling poems learned in school.

Sixteen years old: an explosion of physical strength, adjusting the saddle and toeclips, incomparable joy to be able to ride ever faster, higher, further, longer. Hoping against hope that Louison Bobet—my hero—would win the Tour de France. A touch of disdain for the motorists, slumped in their metal boxes when it is so beautiful outdoors! Unabashed satisfaction to see the muscles firming up, and discreet pleasure to note the lowering of the pulse rate on awakening in the morning in the sun-filled room at the youth hostel. The audacity to break the 100, the 200, and then right after the 300 km barrier in one stretch. All of France crossed with a few strokes of the pedals, rhythm in my legs, daydreams in my head. Awe of dawn after a nocturnal start, following the banks of the Loire. Enthusiastic confrontation with the mountains—the higher the climb, the stronger the emotions. And that first unforgettable 150km time trial, feet locked in the toeclips, nose to the stem, body launched, an arrow flying like a lover to a tryst.

Eighteen years old: fiendish laps around the track at Long-champ, mingling with the real racers, on a bicycle weighing 15 kilos with half balloon tires.

Twenty-two years old: buying my first racing bike at the avenue de la Grande-Armée, going right to the top of the line with my first paycheck. And just the right price.

Let's stop there!

I have loved bicycling all my life.

Louison Bobet at the height of his career in 1954: breaking away in the Alps, he completely dominated the Tour de France.

technical details

The editor thanks the Bernard Tapie Sport and Cycles Lejeune companies for having loaned the equipment needed to write this book. He also thanks Wes Coggins and Bernard Chene for the detailed information they furnished us on the products made by their companies and which we present on the following pages.

- **The bike which won the Tour of Italy, the Tour de France, the Tour of Sweden, and the Coors International Classic in 1985**

The bike that Bernard Hinault and his La Vie Claire teammates use is sold by Look at Nevers.
You can own this bike, just as it is used for racing:
- Reynolds 753 steel frame
- Campagnolo Record cranks, bottom bracket, pedals, brakes, derailleurs, and hubs
- Cinelli bars and stem
- San Marco (Rools) saddle
- Ambrosio rims
- Maillard freewheel
- Sedis chain
- Alsthom fiber and Mica Disc Jet lenticular wheel
- Vittoria tires
- Look pedals

For more information contact the customer service department of Look, rue de la Pique, B.P. 72, 58004 Nevers Cedex, France.

- **"Lend me your bike, Bernard?"**

Everyone dreams of asking Bernard Hinault this question. That's why the Badger had the idea of creating a bike which resembles his, without being exactly the same. The goal was to make this bike available to everyone, while maintaining the quality, the finish, and the style which would compare to professionals' machines.

This is the Colorado, painted gray with red trim and chrome forks. The frame is made of three Reynolds tubes, the water bottle cage and shift levers are brazed on, and the rear dropouts have an adjustment screw which helps center the wheel. The fork crown is very sloping, and the stays are brazed directly to the seat tube joint, which gives the bike a very modern look. The other main characteristics of the Colorado are:

- duraluminum brakes, arms with springs, drilled levers
- pedal ensemble with a square shaft and duraluminum removable cranks and chainrings
- aero pedals with adjustable toeclips
- duraluminum 12-speed front and rear derailleurs with aero levers
- 36-hole hubs
- freewheel with removable caps
- chrome spokes
- duraluminum 36-hole rims with eyelets
- racing sew-ups
- duraluminum handlebars
- grooved duraluminum seat post and saddle
- leather-covered saddle
- chrome pump
- 50 to 62 cm frame height

Bernard Hinault has also considered the wider public in creating a line of 15 models, including racing, sport, cyclocross and all-terrain, as well as a women's model. These bicycles are only available at specialized stores where there is someone to advise the buyer. Thus the prestigious name of Bernard Hinault will be rolling on all the roads of France as well as beyond the French borders.

Two models are especially dear to Bernard Hinault: the Lady Martine, which carries his wife's first name, and the Brittany, which represents his birthplace. The Lady Martine is a women's bike, with a mixte frame. It has 3 speeds, duraluminum brakes, 2 luggage carriers, half balloon tires, a light, and a kickstand. It comes in two colors, pearly blue and pearly white, which Bernard Hinault wanted to be luminescent. The Brittany belongs to the generation of new machines called mountain bikes. Bernard Hinault himself has one, which he uses to ride around in the Breton countryside to loosen up. Most of the parts of the Brittany are duraluminum. The reinforced frame carries the colors of the rainbow jersey, a jersey Bernard Hinault knows well, since he was a world champion. Equipped with 18 speeds to master all terrain, this bike has a chainring protector and studded tires.

Information on request:
Cycles Lejeune
11 to 25 av. du General-Leclerc
94704 Maisons-Alfort cedex
France
Tel: (1) 43.68.36.10

index